With Best Wishes

James Brodie

My Hunting England
James Barclay

This edition published 2015 by Ruddocks Publishing Limited, Lincoln.
ISBN 978 0 904327 23 6

Printed by Ruddocks
56 Great Northern Terrace, Lincoln LN5 8HL

CONTENTS

LIST OF SUBSCRIBERS

Mr and Mrs Stuart Smith

Mr and Mrs Arthur Lockwood

Mr and Mrs John Lockwood

Miss Jill Taylor

Ms Bridget Fox

Mrs Rosemary O'Shea

Mr Michael Mcnulty

Mr Frank Fortescue

Mr Nicholas Turner

Ms Sally Hughes

Mr and Mrs Steve Little

Col and Mrs Nick Foster

Ms Mary Ewing

Miss Margaret Hogger

Mr and Mrs Terry Pinner

Mrs Jane Tuckwell

Mr Jos Mottershead

Mr and Mrs William Craven

Mr Jeremy Scott Bolton

Ms Judith Leman

Mr John Edwards

Mr Bryan Pye

Mr Trevor Marks

Mr and Mrs Jim Meads

Mr Mark Dudley

Ms Sophie Howard

Ms Susan Harris

Mr Foster Edwards

Dedicated to my Great Grandfather, Grandfather and Father,
all of whom committed their lives to the good of hunting and the English countryside.

AN INTRODUCTION TO MY HUNTING ENGLAND

The title of this book My Hunting England may seem to some as though I am being somewhat arrogant by presuming that Hunting England is all about me! I can assure you it is not and it is my sincere hope that as the thread of the book becomes clear, you will see the role that our family have played in the sport is somewhat minor compared to the many who have given so freely of their time to ensure that hunting is still here despite everything that has been thrown at it over the years, especially since that dreaded day in February 2005. The fabric of our sport is very much intact and this is down to all those who have kept the belief and refused to capitulate. They are unsung heroes, many of whom you will read about later, some are sadly no longer with us, others are and still very much up for the battle for common sense to prevail.

Most of those in our family have thought of little else other than hunting for a long time now. So my father, thought that I, as his youngest son, should go off and find a worthwhile occupation, like becoming a Vicar. However I had other plans in mind and if I could not have an involvement with my family pack I would go and find a pack of my own. This is what I did and what a particular pleasure it has all been. It is the people who I have met and worked with from every corner of society that have made everything so worthwhile. When you add to that, the packs of hounds I have either been fortunate enough to hunt, hunt with or be their Master you will see how it becomes such an all engrossing subject.

Throughout my life my family and I have been surrounded by good people with whom we have shared not only our love of hunting England but every aspect of rural life that fits so naturally into it.

This book is split into four sections, the first covering from my childhood memories up to the time I was hunting the Essex and Suffolk. We will then go on to follow the lives of those who are our unsung heroes some of whom are still contributing hugely to our every day way of life. There are many more whom could so easily be fitted in to this category but there has not been enough room to do so in this book. The next part is something that is often talked about but will never be understood and that is the strange happenings that so often occur after the death of some of our many friends, who have shared an interest in the life we know so well. To this end I am extremely grateful to Tony Wright, the Huntsman of the Exmoor who will tell us what happened exactly a year to the day after Captain Wallace died; Colin Stephenson who whipped in to the Pytchley for many years relates in detail what happened at the Cottesmore Kennels after the tragic death of Herbert Norman and I am extremely grateful to Joe Cowen the long time Master of the Fernie for sharing with us two of his family's stories. Lastly it has been an honour to be asked to write about those people who have sadly gone on to the other place and really left their mark on us. I therefore have included those obituaries I have been entrusted to write.

It is my hope you will very much enjoy the content of this book. It has taken longer than I anticipated to produce as a conscious decision was made to illustrate it all with my own photographs. This has very largely been achieved but I owe a great debt of gratitude to Jim Meads for his generosity for allowing us to include his photos of those who were about before I took up photography. Lastly our thanks to Judith Leman, our great friend from Australia who has so very kindly produced the charming sketches for us.

FOREWORD

I feel very honoured by James Barclay to be asked to write a short foreword to this, his first book. My family and the Barclay family have been friends for many years, commencing I believe, when my father, Sir Peter Farquhar, started hunting hounds in the early 1920`s, and was helped out with advice on hound breeding by James's grandfather, Major Mo Barclay, who was already a senior and time honoured Master and huntsman of the Puckeridge.

Indeed his son, Captain Charles Barclay, James's father had been a friend of my family since the end of the second world war, and he himself was a celebrated Master and huntsman, hound breeder and foxhound judge. It was not surprising therefore that James, who I have known since he was a young boy, should inherit a passionate and enthusiastic love of hounds and the chase which also led him into a successful career in both breeding and hunting hounds.

One of James's greatest attributes has been his ability to think outside the box, and from an early age he was wise enough to realise that hunting is in fact a very broad church, and that within hunting there are individuals from every walk of life, from the grandest to the lowest, who all have a common bond, and James has capitalised on this wherever he has been Master. He also realised that this was a light and a message that should not be hidden and he has always tried to explain this to the outside world. He was as well, wise enough to notice, that in the 80`s and 90`s the hunting world was not good at spreading this gospel both to the media, to politicians, the general public and further afield. He was largely the instigator of the inspired move to persuade teachers and pupils from inner city schools to come out into the countryside to meet hounds and see rural trades, crafts and farming practices at first hand for themselves and the success of what became the countryside Foundation was for the most part his brain child.

It is not surprising therefore that this book also includes interesting eulogies of foxhunters from all over the social spectrum - famous Masters, professional huntsman, earth stoppers and helpers (sad how things have changed). I took great pleasure in reading it and I look forward to the sequel which I am told is likely to include some further interesting detail on the hound and the true art of venery.

I hope you enjoy it.

Capt. Ian Farquhar
Joint Master of the Duke of Beaufort's
Vice Chairman of the MFHA

INTRODUCTION

James has as much hunting blood running through his veins as anyone living and a Puckeridge pedigree to match. I was fortunate to be able to persuade his father, Captain Charlie Barclay, in the mid 1970's, that James would advance his career by coming to The Warwickshire Foxhounds, and working as my PR assistant, alias fencer, earth stopper and general 'boy-of-no-account'. He did me proud, forging excellent relationships with all landowners and farmers; even those whose enthusiasm for welcoming fields of 100+ across their land needed a little uplifting! He and I worked as a team and my job was made very much easier, especially if there happened to be a drama during the hunting day. We continued our team work when I transferred to The Heythrop in 1982. James lived at the kennels and played a major role in the running of a busy four days/week pack.

He helped foster warm relations with all the drivers who manned the local Worcester-Oxford train service and who always had a strong presence at our earth stoppers' and keepers' dinner. One of the railway men invited him for a trip in the driver's cab one day and, as the train pulled up at Charlbury station, James hailed one of our senior hunting land owners, who was waiting on the platform. The shock of seeing JB apparently driving the train was too much and caused the much respected sportsman to have a stroke shortly afterwards (happily, he recovered).

James has a special talent for making everyone feel part of the community. This is a rare and invaluable gift. I was so fortunate to have his assistance, support, humour and friendship for so many years of my career. The hunting world has been well served by many Barclays, and James' contribution has been up with the best of that family.

Stephen Lambert

Stephen Lambert.
Chairman of the MFHA 2005-2014

A TRIBUTE TO MY VULPINE FRIENDS

With over two hundred years of Mastership of various packs of Hounds under our belt, you will understand it was and always will be the number one rule in the Barclay family, to have the greatest respect for our quarry species, be it the fox, deer or hare. The pleasure all three give is immense and it is in the watching, not only on a hunting day but during the lazy days of summer when I find them equally fascinating.

Whist the others are without doubt of equal interest, it is the fox that has taken up a very large part of my time and a day does not pass, when he doesn't enter my mind in one way or another. It is more than likely he will be discussed at some point, especially when he is being blamed for eating someone's prime poultry. Whenever, they are talked about however, it is normally with quite a large degree of affection, except of course, on the day a heinous crime has been acted out, in his role as the ruthless killer.

The pleasure in writing this has been to remember in detail the moments when my vulpine friends have behaved in an extraordinary way. Several incidents will always be etched in my mind and I realise how fortunate I am to have these memories. In the past I have recollected their somewhat strange behaviour after the death of a particularly well known sporting character. This you will see is not quite the same although there are places where the two do join forces which certainly leaves me wondering.

Growing up in Hertfordshire at Brent Pelham was I believe a privilege. It was a place where we learnt so much about wildlife and how to appreciate the beautiful countryside in which we lived. The Puckeridge Hounds played an all absorbing part of my life, as did the farm and everything that went with it. During harvest as the combines rolled on, my father thoroughly enjoyed taking us to strategic places where we would count the foxes coming flying out of his fields and to watch carefully as they disappeared in all directions. At the end of each

day the drivers were always asked what they had seen and it was then that a reckoning up would take place as to what was about and where they were likely to have gone. This was not through any potential blood lust, it was a dedicated fascination of the animal which played a rather important part in our lives. At night when the hounds were not singing in kennels, more often it would be the foxes keeping us awake by barking away around the house. At breakfast the next morning it was always a point for discussion about who had heard what. So with this sort of upbringing the vulpine species, you will understand, was hardly going to disappear from my mind.

One experience which still stands out a mile was whilst I was with Clarence Webster at the Warwickshire, working as a rather inefficient kennel

It says it all

boy in the seventies. It was in early February and there had been a light fall of snow during the night. We had gone into the kennels as normal at six and washed down. Clarence always walked the dog hounds and the bitches out separately, and on this particular morning we went into the back field with the old boys. After half an hour or so we were back and getting ready to take out the next lot when Clarence asked if I would nip up to the slaughter house and get some flesh for the first feed. When I got there, I could scarcely believe my eyes. There on a mound, no more than twenty yards from me was a fox mooching about without a care in the world. Not only that, wherever the old dog hounds had cocked their legs, he was doing the same.

In my very early days at the Essex and Suffolk a former very enthusiastic shooting farmer rang me up to say he had found a litter of cubs and would I like to pop over, have some supper with him and go out and watch them for a while. Of course my answer was yes and what a treat was in store for me, there they all were lying out on some winter wheat. Within a second of hearing us they were gone and for the next forty minutes nothing appeared, despite being in exactly the right place for the wind. Who could blame them? It would seem as though we were not likely to witness any further action, when suddenly out of the blue a well grown cub appeared, followed by another and another until all five were no more than twenty yards away from where we were sitting. Then the old vixen appeared and made her way out into the shadows where we could see her keeping a watchful eye on proceedings. After witnessing all the rough and tumble of these young foxes at play, my farmer friend placed a pot of honey in my hand and whispered to me to go down flat on the ground and squeak like a rabbit in distress. Taking my orders this is exactly what I did. I could never have expected what was to happen next though. I saw this cub advancing cautiously towards me and thought to myself what the dickens is happening here, then suddenly I felt the weight of his pad on my hand and saw him looking at me straight in the eye whilst he licked the honey off my finger. This was an experience, I would have never thought possible. These were wild foxes that had hardly seen a human being before and for one to actually do this, was just extraordinary. I still cannot believe it happened and we often talk about it all these years later. Billy Shipp, the farmer who organised the whole exercise, was a true countryman in the finest sense, as was his colleague Alfred Jennings, a neighbouring farmer who was with us that night. They both gave up shooting to partake in the activities of the Essex and Suffolk Hunt and it was through them the word balance became so important to me, not only in creating an understanding of the fox but to find ways for the two sports to work together. Sadly the pair of them have now gone on to the other place, however they certainly had an impact on me in how to run a pack of hounds, in a shooting country.

Anyway, it was when I joined the Fitzwilliam Mastership and my wife Lucy and I moved into our first marital home in Milton Park, near Peterborough, that really strange happenings began to occur. At that time Milton was the home of the Fitzwilliam family but is now in the hands of the Naylor-Leylands. The Hounds are the descendants of those many famous ones whose breeding goes right back to the mid 1700's and beyond. To see foxes in the Park was not unusual particularly round the Kennels, however on

Eye to Eye

one particular night I was awoken by two animals fighting under our bedroom window. Lucy had a rather large ginger cat at the time and my immediate thought was it was the neighbouring tom come up for a scrap with his mate. Not a bit of it. There, just under the window were two foxes locked in battle. I put my head out and asked them in quite a loud voice, what they were doing waking us up like this. At first it made not the slightest bit of difference, but then after a while they drew back from one another, looked up at the window and started cackling at me. This unusual behaviour went on for a good three minutes or so, before the pair of them decided to slink quietly away into the covert beside the house, and they were gone. They obviously had their minds on other things and were not worried about me being in the vicinity that was for certain.

A few years later we moved to the village of Southorpe, not many miles from Milton. Our two sons were growing up fast and a little more room was needed. It was on our very first night there that we were woken again by a similar but now very recognisable noise. This time though, it was a bit more muffled. So, heaving oneself out of bed and with a torch in hand, I proceeded to shine it down onto the drive below. Well I could hardly believe my eyes. There were three old foxes all piling into each other in what I can only describe as the mother and father of all battles. They took not the slightest notice of me, so I decided after a while to go back to bed and leave them to it. The next morning, there was the Head Keeper from the Walcot Estate, Jeff Davey on the doorstep. "Brought the foxes with you then, have you?" he laughed. He had been on night watch duty and had witnessed just what I had, except when he stopped and shone the headlights on them they cleared off in all directions.

After twelve very happy seasons at the Fitzwilliam, we relocated to the Cottesmore, deciding to build a house on a neglected piece of land in the old railway village of Little Bytham, just north of Stamford. As the works came to an end there was a considerable amount of topsoil left over so we decided to bank it up and plant it with shrubs, bulbs and wildflowers. It was on a Sunday morning and I was busy digging away when all of a sudden something caught my eye, a hundred yards away under the gate to the top paddock came Charlie. Down the field he trotted until he was five yards away from me and that is where he stopped still, he and I stared at each other without stirring. My old dog lay on the bank beside me and never once went to see him off. This was strange to say the least. After what seemed about fifty minutes but was more like five, he decided to make his move, not away but came over to within a yard of me. He then suddenly put his nose in the air, made his way up the field again, and was gone.

Sadly after Lucy's first horrific accident in the village, we had to move as adapting the house for her would not have been possible. So off up to the middle of Lincolnshire it was to take on the South Wold Hounds. We found a beautiful old fashioned farm house in the village of Stixwould near Woodhall Spa. It would seem as though we had not been there five minutes when there was a knock at the door. It was our immediate neighbour. He proceeded to tell me he and his wife could not believe what they had seen the night before. They were on their way home late in the evening when they came across a very large fox standing in the middle of the road right outside our gate, who on being disturbed decided to trot straight up our drive virtually to the back door. This I have to say was pretty extraordinary as foxes at that time were a rare sight in this part of Lincolnshire. However it is what has followed on from this occasion that makes these happenings all the more peculiar, whether at home at Stixwould or elsewhere.

Unexpected encounters continued to take place and on the 19th November 2013 there was one in particular which brought it all very close to home. I had travelled down to Brent Pelham for a ninetieth birthday party, arriving in the village at half past three in the afternoon. As I turned down beside the Church to go to the

Judith A. Leman

The Blankney Fox

Puckeridge Kennels, there for all to see was a fox sitting perfectly calmly on the verge right opposite the graves of my father, mother and many of my forebears. Nothing unusual in that one might say, but where he sat was exactly the same place as where we had stopped with the Puckeridge Hounds just a month or two before to remember both our parents.

In February of this year the Blankney met at Lake Farm, Washingborough, near Lincoln and with birds of prey in place the hounds went up to draw a thick patch of thorns above a large expanse of black fenland. The covert is largely surrounded by a moat and I made my way through to a spot where I hoped I might see some action. Sure enough it wasn't to be long before it all began to happen, right in front of me. I went to stand with Philip Stubbings the Huntsman when after a while he pointed towards the water's edge. There was the fox, just in the middle of launching himself into the water. Luckily with camera in hand I managed to take five wonderful shots of him, the last of which was probably one of the most special I have ever taken. As he was about three or four yards from landing he suddenly changed direction and swam straight towards us. Then, seemingly treading water for a few seconds he turned away, landed on the opposite bank, shook himself and again like all the others was gone.

For many years I had a wonderful terrier called Murphy who would go out at night and if there was a fox about, would bark at it until he or she would disappear. Murphy sadly died in March 2014 and is buried under our bedroom window. A few days later the South Wold Hounds met here for the last day of the season and I asked their Master and Huntsman if he would just stand beside the grave and just for a minute, blow for the old dog. After all he and I had done many a mile together hunting with numerous packs of hounds around the country and it felt most appropriate. A sad occasion, however a few weeks later, Poiteen his son, shot out of the door late one evening and started barking like you would not believe. I went round the corner of the house and there under the outside light were two of our vulpine friends fighting on the old dog's grave. They were soon seen off but

My Old Friend Murphy

'Yonder he goes'

over the next two hours kept returning to bate the young fellar. Eventually all three of them ended up piling into each other outside the front door. Three weeks later they were back and the same scene was played out all over again, this time though keeping me on my toes until gone half past three in the morning.

Whilst I am sure there will be be many who have experienced similar incidents, I personally feel these amazing events have been absolutely extraordinary. Is there so much more out there that we are unaware of which can make things like this happen? If anybody has an answer please let me know, it cannot all just be coincidence, or can it?

It is the word 'respect' that we proudly talk about which exists in the majority of hunting people, between us and our quarry species that is so important, whoever they are and from whatever background they come. We must never let go of it, for doing so would bring disastrous consequences.

MY EARLY LIFE

From a Hospital Bed

Whilst lying in a hospital bed on the night of 30th April 2012, it very soon became apparent that my time at the sharp end of hunting was up. I had decided six months before that living in Lincolnshire and being Master of a pack of hounds in Nottinghamshire was just too much. Little did I realise at the time, for the next ten days I would be reflecting back on 36 years' involvement with this most wonderful sport and the people with whom I had been privileged to work. I needed some luck to help me write this article and that luck came, believe it or not, from a rather large influx of genuine hunting, farming types who happened not only to be in the same hospital, but on the same ward for similar procedures as myself. It was, without any doubt, the company that made my stay there rather more pleasurable than it would have been. What the nurses thought of us, God only knows, but I do know they were very good to us and didn't make us suffer.

In a situation like this, you have to make the best of life and, would you believe it, whilst just chatting to my fellow inmates it wasn't long before the name Wallace happened to come into a conversation. My father always said he got everywhere. Then Colonel Mitchell of Hambledon fame, then Jim Webster, Michael Farrin etc. etc. and on it went. There we were stuck in the City Hospital, in the middle of Nottingham and all these great names from the past kept popping up. It certainly stopped us from worrying about our own health or potential heart surgery. Then came the morning of my procedure and on the way down to theatre, would you believe it, there was one of the South Notts and Grove and Rufford's most loyal farmers and supporters having his breakfast, so I paid him the compliments of the morning. On returning to a new ward little did I expect to find him in the adjoining bed. Well that didn't help. You could not get away from them. We were in full cry for the next week.

I mentioned earlier how the well known names in hunting came up in conversation. What a debt of gratitude we owe them, for the standard of sport they set, the hounds they bred and for keeping hunting going in one form or another throughout two World Wars. They willingly passed on their knowledge to us younger ones, with a kindness and generosity of spirit for which they were not always acknowledged. I clearly remember sitting beside the fire at Brent Pelham with Lord Knutsford teaching me how to play *D'ye Ken John Peel* on the hunting horn.

In a sporting magazine I had recently been reading there was an article about the great Masters and Huntsmen the writer had known and rated the best. Many of the names he mentioned you would probably expect to be there; they deserved the full credit they received. However I believe the time has come to pay tribute to the Huntsmen, both amateur and professional, of the 21st century who face many challenges that those hunting in the last century would never have thought possible. Behind every good Huntsman lies a good Mastership and without the two working together the set up is doomed to failure. It is where mutual respect is the key ingredient. The knowledge of the country, its farmers and the people who live and work there are the priority. Passing back this information to their Huntsman will inevitably make his job much easier. From that not only will the hounds benefit, the sport will improve and hard riding will be needed to keep up with them. There will be no time for larking. The key to success is centred round one word and that is Communication with a capital C. If there is none, it is the hunt and those who have been loyal to it, some for many generations, who will suffer. Great unrest is something we can well do without nowadays.

So with all this in mind and free of all responsibilities I set out to see what had been going on in and around the eastern side of the country and the Shires. With the wettest summer on record and possibly one of the wettest autumns, it was far from easy for anybody. However the standards that I was most fortunate to witness from the fifteen packs visited was undeniably outstanding. The commitment to slog it out and keep going as well as they can until this ridiculous piece of legislation can be repealed has been very much in evidence. So to all who are at the sharp end of hunting today, be proud of the considerable efforts you are making to show good sport, be proud of your hounds and most of all enjoy it.

Commitment and Communication

As I progressed on my tour around the country, the deep willed commitment to keep going in one form or another was still very much in evidence. It is to be applauded at the very highest degree and will stand us in good stead for the future. Despite the challenges that lie ahead, the feeling of true grit is, I am delighted to say, out there in bucket loads. Something else which is a real pleasure to see in these most difficult times, or at any time for that matter, is that there really are some lovely hounds about. Where would we be without them?

The old words of 'andsom is as 'andsom does, may very well be true, but I remember talking to Captain Wallace many years ago. He was sitting with his Hounds at Warren Gate after a long morning and we were discussing various members of the rather good looking lot that surrounded him. He said something in his own distinctive way, which I shall never forget. "You can have an ugly pack of hounds, James, and they will hunt

their heart out for you. You can have a beautiful pack of hounds and they won't hunt a yard. However," he went on, "it is rather nice to get the combination of both isn't it?" There he was sitting high up on Exmoor having just had a decent morning, catching a brace and yes, looking at them, he had achieved exactly that. Wise words for a young man.

The Captain and my father were very close in age and happened to be at school together. A place otherwise named Slough Grammar School, which also used to keep a rather well known pack of Beagles. This is probably where the rivalry began. Whilst they had the utmost respect for each other, they did remind me of two jealous old dog hounds who would make out they could not agree over anything. They judged numerous puppy shows together throughout the land, but sadly age did weary them and the double act came to an end after many years. However, they will not be forgotten. I will remember both of them for the sheer tenacity in hunting the fox. They always said that my old Dad could read what his quarry was going to do next. I believe they were both extremely fortunate to have this gift and more than likely had an idea where the feller they were pursuing was going, before he even had time to cock his leg.

"Those were the days! Far better than it is today!" Maybe, as the world has changed, and some may say what is hunting still doing here? It is here because it has adapted to 21st Century life. Yes it had to but it has not lost its overall standards, which really does make our critics angry. It is something of which everybody involved in hunting today should be extremely proud. We have not only demonstrated our greatest strength, survival in the face of adversity, we have shown true resilience and guts.

Where does this strength of resolve come from? It is without any doubt, in the British spirit. However let us just cast back to the beginning of this article and later the conversation with Captain Wallace. These demonstrate, in different ways, a sense of commitment which cannot be questioned. It is that, and more, which is directly and indirectly rubbing off positively on all those involved in hunting today and coming from the many other sections of society who have generously rallied behind our cause. These reasons are mostly why we are still here today. Boxing Day and New Year's Day are the two days of the year that prove just how popular hunting really is. Bawtry, South Yorkshire last year proved this in an area which is not entirely rural.

By bringing this Commitment together with first class Communication, we have the key to our future. Communicating positively to the outside world, as well as between ourselves, is a vital ingredient. Being ready to act quickly when something goes wrong, if you and your hounds end up in an embarrassing situation, it is equally important. This was nicely demonstrated by a rather enthusiastic Master some years ago, when his hounds ran through several gardens. The result of this unfortunate incident was seventy or so townsfolk visiting the kennels for a specially arranged Open Morning to meet the Hunt Staff and hounds and find out more about our activities. This could not have been a greater success.

So there we have it, with the two C words working in harmony, hunting will be as ever ready to fight off the enemy. Most importantly though, it will always be there to win new friends.

Early Days

Having had an incredibly lucky life I thought maybe it might be of interest to share some of it with you and if you didn't mind I will turn the clock back to the beginning and see if we can find where this obsession with hunting came from.

The Puckeridge Hounds in front of the house where I was born

So from where has it all materialised? If you are breeding hounds, the expert Martin Scott will wisely advise you to look at the many different characteristics of the forebears before deciding the plan ahead, i.e. nose, drive, cry, stamina, colour, looks etc. Look back at the tail male and tail female lines and there will lie many, but not all, the answers you are looking for, which of course makes it all so interesting. They say the female line is the more important. So for example if you were to investigate the breeding of a particular individual and his family, some of his characteristics and conformation are, as you would expect, evident on both lines, noticeably being too big and of course an enthusiasm for the chase. Although colour is not a crucial factor in many cases, it is most interesting, be it in canines, equines, homo sapiens or any other species, how it comes out. It is fascinating to me then, to look at our own tail female line. It is here that we find our four greats grandmother, to be a Jamaican lady, called Mary Finney. We always wondered why certain members of the Barclay and Slingsby families came out a little darker in colour to others, and I am proud to say it came from her and it is still in evidence today.

My great grandfather who achieved fifty one seasons as Master, had already died when I was born in the late '50s. My Grandfather was fast approaching his fiftieth season, and Dad had already completed twelve of his fifty-five, so as you can imagine, there was little chance to really do anything else with one's life however hard one tried. My very early memories are of hunting on the fabulous Judy, a donkey that had been in the family for ever and served all four of us and others besides. On our first day it was tradition for us to wear a small version of a scarlet coat which had been made for my Great Grandfather and has been worn by each member of the family since, including my own two sons on their first day's hunting.

Photograph by Jim Meads

1963 on Judy

What an amazing place I had in which to grow up. Brent Pelham was, and still is, a place where farming and foxhunting are inextricably linked. It was somewhere which taught me from a very early age the important values of what the rural community really stood for. It was a place where the very core of goodwill not only thrived, but flourished and was also where the words of Lord Willoughby de Broke in 1927 came to life.

"Hunting, for it to survive, must be totally and utterly inclusive. If not it loses its very reason for being there." Of course there are many other estates throughout the country, such as Badminton, Brocklesby and Milton which are very similar, but Brent Pelham has a particular charm of its own, probably because it is somewhat smaller and has farming, rather than estate management, at its very root.

Brent Pelham came into the family after Great Grandfather had decided to leave the family Bank. Some would say that this might have been an unwise move, however working in the City certainly was not his forte and one has to remember that hunting was extremely important to him. From being a very young man he kept his own private pack of harriers kennelled at Roydon, on the edge of what is now North London, and hunted in places that you could never even in your wildest nightmares consider going to today. Imagine hacking your hounds through Tottenham to the station where they would be put on the train to Suffolk or Norfolk for their annual hunting holiday. When he was not hunting his harriers he was hunting with the Essex Foxhounds. He became Master of the Puckeridge in 1896. So there you are. That in a nutshell is how the family's involvement in hunting was born.

In 1962 changes were made to the breeding of the Puckeridge Hounds. Grandfather and Dad sat down one day for lunch and decided that to improve their size they would start to integrate some Beaufort blood into them, and initial contact should be made with the 10th Duke who was, until his death in 1985, a close family friend. Until this time they had been totally pure English and always went to Brocklesby or Belvoir for Stallion Hounds and it saddened them to have to go elsewhere but change there had to be. There was nothing in any way whatsoever wrong with their working capabilities, they were just beginning to get smaller and an outcross had to be found. It must have had a devastating effect on my Grandfather, because later that afternoon he dropped dead in the garden at Brent Pelham, on his way back from his regular afternoon walk to the Kennels. A neighbouring farmer, who happened to be named Ernie Fox, told me how he had seen him shortly before his sudden death. My Grandfather recounted the decision that my father and he had made that morning to change the breeding of his beloved hounds. He was so upset about this that he hit a pebble 50 yards up the road with his walking stick, in spite of him being nearly blind. Twenty minutes later he was dead leaving a gap in the Mastership for my mother to fill. So it was left to them to implement the changes that had been discussed just a few hours earlier.

Badminton, School and Amalgamations

As the influence of the Duke of Beaufort's brood bitches Woeful and Worry and his Stallion Hounds, Beadle, Crowner and others grew on the breeding of the Puckeridge Hounds, so did the importance of it all on the mind of this, the youngest member of the family. With wonderful ponies to hunt and a most enthusiastic mother who was now a Joint Master with Dad, the excitement and pleasure of it all was really beginning to take hold, as it so obviously had done with the previous members of the family. When not hunting, many an afternoon was spent either in the Kennels with the legendary Ned Paxton who had been 1st Whipper In and Kennel Huntsman since the War or later with Ron Quarmby who came from the HH (Hampshire Hunt). Ron did a tremendous job in supporting Dad's improvements to the hounds. The school holidays were also spent earth stopping with the well known Terrier Men of their time, Ken Hand, David Morse and latterly Vernon Taney. What all these chaps taught me about the fox became invaluable to me later in life. I will always be indebted to them.

It was late in the summer of 1967 that the family received an invitation to go and stay at Badminton for a few days cubhunting. His Grace had retired from hunting the hounds the season before and Brian Gupwell was

Badminton House

at the sharp end having recently arrived from the Eridge. To be invited to Badminton was a young hunting person's dream and I still am very lucky to have the most vivid memories of the whole trip and those that came after. The Duke and Duchess treated us as if we were their own grandchildren. We were given cracking ponies to ride and, when we weren't hunting, were pursuing things other than the vulpine species around the garden with the Duke's dogs, which caused great amusement not only to us youngsters, but the Duke as well.

After returning from the West country we would start hunting at home a few days later. Fifty plus couple of hounds would stream out of the Puckeridge Kennels for the first morning and with the whole family out, it did rather demonstrate the eccentric enthusiasm the Barclays have for the sport. As was the case after hunting at Badminton, a huge breakfast would be there for us on our return thus giving you a further indication why some members of the family are, or were, far larger than they should have been.

Academia was never my strongest point so you can imagine when the time came to go to Boarding School in the autumn of 1968 there was quite a rebellion from this one, who at the time was only nine years old. It was especially upsetting as more than likely we would have just returned from Badminton and Cubhunting was getting underway at home. Summer Fields, Oxford was the chosen place for my education. This was an institution where many of the top MFH's and MP's were educated before going onto Eton, Harrow or another top notch school. Not for me. Within two years I was out of there, to somewhere much more suitable in the heart of the Grafton country.

This brings us up to the year of 1970, one which will be remembered for two important amalgamations. The Puckeridge and Newmarket and Thurlow came together to make a big four day a week country, hunting in Hertfordshire, Essex, Cambridgeshire and Suffolk. At the same time the Hertfordshire, Old Berkeley, and South

Photograph by Jim Meads

My brothers and I with Mother and Father at the Opening Meet 1967

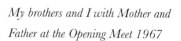

Oxfordshire joined forces to make an even larger country adjoining the newly formed Puckeridge and Thurlow. They became the Vale of Aylesbury and continued to wear the mustard livery of the Old Berkeley with the charming Jim Bennett hunting the hounds. Whilst all this was going on efforts were being made to give me some form of education. I was trying my hardest but at the same time I couldn't resist asking Mr Perry the Headmaster if he would give a Meet at the School. After a considerable amount of negotiation the answer thankfully was yes, and it was not many months later that Col Foster, Captain Hawkins, Joe Miller and the Grafton Hounds were hacking up the school drive. This was Joe's last season and what a delightful man he was. He was one of the finest examples of the old school and it is a privilege to have known him. I used to see him occasionally at Puppy Shows after he retired but he rarely went hunting. He was fearful that people would say he was only there to criticise the new regime, although I have to say that was not in the man's nature. He was a fine example of the true gentleman that Hunt Service often produces.

Tommy Normington came to the Grafton the following season from the Tynedale. He was another one from the highest league of professionals. Tommy had been brought up at the Fitzwilliam where his father was Stud Groom. It was here that he and Brian Pheasey both served under the great disciplinarian Jack Simister, who was described as being very firm but fair. At this time Jack's brother, Dick hunted the Cowdray and was renowned for having a tremendous rapport with his hounds, which was hugely important, as it was a country full of deer.

The Grafton met at the School again that year, but to me it was not quite the same. Somebody was missing who had been there the previous year. Mother had died just a few weeks before, leaving a gaping hole in all our lives. She had been diagnosed with terminal cancer, having just returned from our annual trip to Badminton. She was Joint Master of the Puckeridge for only ten seasons with Dad, but her achievements were quite outstanding. Our memory of her will always be of her encouraging us and numerous young to go out, crack on, and enjoy our hunting. Not long before she died she helped me set up a pack called the Barclay Rabbit Hounds which gave us all tremendous fun during the school holidays and lasted right up until 1976. On a recent visit back to the Puckeridge country a very loyal and senior car follower came over and remarked: "James what about the good old days of the Rabbit Hounds?" Happy memories indeed.

The Rabbit Hounds, Schooling and first Employment

With my dear Mother having sadly gone on to another place, our idea about the Rabbit Hounds continued to go from strength to strength and I can only hope she would have been proud of us. After all she had laid the foundation stones for a future Master, which is something I shall be eternally grateful for, although I am not sure if the pocket has been.

Great inspiration at the time also came from Jack Ivester Lloyd who wrote regular articles in the Shooting Times about the exploits of the Bagley Rabbit Hounds (BRH) which hunted in Shropshire. Meanwhile at home the country was opened up, and during the school holidays we were out on the three days in the week that the newly amalgamated Puckeridge and Thurlow were not out. This included the Sunday, after Church of course. New Masters were appointed, and Hunt supporters' events planned. The BRH received much encouragement in a way which was highly satisfying to all of us mad keen young hunters. To call them Rabbit Hounds was probably a misnomer, as we all know there is no such thing as a Rabbit Hound, so we used anything from the local mongrel to the most highly bred Labrador with anything else in between. They were trencher fed and all individually owned. We would go round the local villages gathering them up and then set sail for our 11.30 am Meet, either at a Pub or some big country House where the poor owner had been press ganged into entertaining us.

Although we called ourselves Rabbit Hunters, if we were in existence today we would probably have been called Law Breakers, as the odd muntjac, fallow buck, hare or even a Puckeridge fox occasionally succumbed to this highly efficient pack of Hertfordshire cur dogs. As a result, keeping Captain Charlie Barclay MFH on side as to where we could hunt was not always the easiest of tasks. Anyway the memory of a Meet at Walkern Hall near Stevenage will last long. A pack of seven and a half couple of mixed hounds had been brought together from all around the county and were accompanied by a field of seventy five. I dare not mention what the tally consisted of that day, but the assembled troupe seemed to enjoy the proceedings to the extent that it is still talked about today. In fact it wasn't long afterwards that the Duke of Beaufort came to stay. He was keen to know how we were progressing with our season and how the lurcher he had given us was working out. I duly told him that all was well and our tally was twenty five brace to date. He said it wasn't too bad, but a certain very well known person he had been staying with in London and who hunted a pack of Corgis and Dorgis (Dachsund x Corgis) had accounted for more than we had. I have to say I think my reply went along the lines that, I thought it was probably easier for them, as they were hunting a country which was surrounded by rather high walls.

So back to school it was. This time it was a new one in the heart of the Hursley country near Romsey in Hampshire, a place where every effort with other kindred spirits was put into forming a pack of Beagles. However this Headmaster was having none of it. We were there to work and achieve good results in our O levels. Some did exactly that, others were not so successful. A way of ensuring that hunting was kept very much on the agenda had to be found. Fortunately our Maths and German teacher Colonel Drew came to the rescue. What a wonderful man he was. He instantly recognised that private tuition would greatly assist in achieving good results in both subjects. Therefore, learning to speak German whilst out with one of the following pack of hounds helped enormously; Hursley, New Forest Foxhounds, New Forest Beagles, Hambledon, Meon Valley Beagles, Palmer Milburn Beagles. Counting hounds is an art in itself and having to do it in German meant I was still being taught in spite of not actually being in the class room. The only pack we were unable to have a day with was the New Forest Buckhounds which I greatly regret. They hunted on Mondays and Fridays, both days which sadly, try as I might, I failed to get off. The venery behind hunting the Fallow Deer must have been fascinating to say the least and I was sorry never to have taken part in it.

The three and a half years after Mother's death until leaving school at sixteen went very quickly and I even narrowly avoided my family giving up on me altogether. So what next?

The Pytchley required a Huntsman. My application for that was turned down for being too young, understandable really! So off to the Blackmore and Sparkford Vale in September 1976 as a rather inefficient 3rd Kennelman / Earth Stopper / Valet. Tony Austin was hunting the hounds. He did not suffer fools gladly but crossed the country like nobody's business. With Tony Herring whipping in to him they showed great sport, be it over the fly fences of the Sparkford Vale or the huge bullfinches of the Blackmore Vale (Ken Anyan had just retired after many years' service). They were in their first season and had a rather mixed lot of hounds to play with, one of which I remember was a huge mottled dog called Crowbar who was by Duke of Beaufort's Crowner. I learnt a lot that season. More than anything to keep your eyes open and wits about you at all times, and as a rather green sixteen year old fresh off the block, to know when to shut up and look sharp. Good advice to anyone who wants to go on and hunt a pack of hounds, it has to be said. So, on it was to pastures new.

An Introduction to Warwickshire

After a brief spell back at Brent Pelham, it was off to the Warwickshire, which as time progressed was to become my second home and given the chance I would happily return as it is a place where I have numerous good friends.

My arrival, a few weeks before the Puppy Show, coincided with filling in the pot holes on the kennel drive, an annual event which took several days, so with a shovel flung into my hand we swiftly got on with the job. Stan Kitchen, who worked in the nearby British Leyland plant at Leamington, was a great friend of my new boss Clarence Webster and he was put in charge of the operation. After several hours of hard graft and a lot of ribbing of the new incumbent, time was called and I was sent off to locate my lodgings. These were with James Way, Master of the Warwickshire Beagles. He was a business partner with Stephen Lambert who, when they were not hunting either the hare or the fox, ran a firm of land agents in Kineton. It was Stephen, then Master of the Warwickshire, who was the one responsible for persuading me to come and work for him, something I greatly enjoyed, and funnily enough not only for the hunting.

Driving up Sun Rising Hill on the Stratford-on-Avon to Banbury road is quite an experience in itself. The view is remarkable and even now thirty five years later sitting at a computer in Lincolnshire, that very first memory is as vivid as ever. It also got me thinking, having been brought up in a very sporting part of Hertfordshire, that it was one of the greatest privileges I could ever have wished for, however London and all that went with it was never far away. This didn't stop the double act of Ned Paxton or latterly Ron Quarmby and Father pulling off some tremendously long and interesting plough country hunts in what was, and is still, an incredibly rural part of the world. I suppose that even in those early days I had the impression that London and its suburbs was where the trouble would come from, and this lay most of the time subconsciously on my mind. Later on when our opponents became more active, I was aware that it was largely caused by the total lack of knowledge that existed and realised that I wanted to try and address this. For now though I was in an equally sporting part of the world but at that time Warwickshire seemed far away from the urban rush.

However finding my base at the very top on Sugarswell Lane and settling myself and my dear old terrier Rusty in was the first priority, then getting ready for a new and most interesting part of my life came next. Two bachelors living in a small cottage, both with a terrier, was an experience to say the least, but on with it we got and good times prevailed.

The Warwickshre Hounds taking a well earned rest

It was at just before six the next morning that I descended Sun Rising Hill for my first day at the kennels. A good looking pack of Warwickshire hounds were there on their yards and it was easy to see even at this young age that I was going to be extremely fortunate to be working with them. In their midst was Grafton who that year had been Champion Dog hound at Peterborough and according to Clarence he had already turned out to be very good in his work. Clarence, whose brother Jim had been at the Belvoir for a number of years, had hunted the Warwickshire for a considerable length of time and was one of the most popular members of his profession. Working with him I learnt so much about the good old fashioned management of hounds and also how important decent manners were and the key to the Hunt being an acceptable part of the local community.

Occasionally the Warwickshire were given raw flesh, however it was more often the case that it was fed cooked, mixed into a wheatmeal pudding. This was something that smelt more than appetising to us young chaps who were working under Clarence, indeed it was lucky that the wages we received were just enough to help us feed ourselves, otherwise it could very easily have been us with our snouts in the troughs. Instead we were all fed by the landlady of the Red Lion in Kineton who for just eighty pence ensured we were given a proper meal at lunchtime. This was ideal and saved a potentially embarrassing situation from arising.

The Puppy Show came and went as did hound exercise and towards the end of August we made a start. However in those intervening months I got to know the hounds and the country in a way which was to become extremely beneficial. Being one of those who collected the fallen stock, or in other words a knackerman, this was a huge advantage in getting to learn my way around. The Warwickshire farmers and the hunt were and still are inextricably linked, and to meet and work with them was a privilege. The importance of the flesh round today is very often underestimated in the good that it can do. It is not just about the feeding of hounds, to me it was the beginnings of learning how to have one's eyes and ears all about the place, as well as one's fingers on the pulse as to what was going on. Because of this I soon got to know a large number of their farmers. Births, deaths and marriages and all the gossip in between could be reported back and if the Masters needed to act they could. So in a short wheel base Land Rover and a long flat trailer attached I would set off on my rounds which covered from Banbury in the East to Stratford-on-Avon in the West, nearly to Rugby in the North and down to Moreton-in-Marsh in the South. It is some of the nicest hunting country imaginable. As a nineteen year old still fresh off the block, I was beginning to see more clearly than ever the benefits of the flesh round. It is my opinion that the strength this link produces is one of the many reasons why in one form or another we are still here, despite our opponents trying as hard as they can to dispose of us. It is where much of our grass roots support has been cultivated and still is today.

Running something like this in the twenty first century is a huge headache and no one understands that more than me. However it does occasionally have its lighter moments and on a very hot Saturday afternoon in the middle of August, I nearly found myself in very hot water. Clarence asked if I would just nip down to the Shipston end of the country and clear up a few smelly sheep before we shut up shop for the weekend. Off I went, and on my way back I thought I would call in and see my father's old friends, Sir John and Lady Wiggin at Honington Hall. I duly pulled up outside the front door as I always had done in the past and walked in to the house and gave them a shout. It was as the odour of maggoty old sheep reached Sir John that I experienced his wrath. "Get that bloody thing round the back and hide it, we are due to open the house to the public in ten minutes", he shouted, from the comfort of his armchair. Sure enough they were and as I sat in the kitchen ten minutes later with Sarah Wiggin having my lunch, the first coach rolled up the drive and a large group of pensioners from Wolverhampton disembarked.

The Warwickshire Hounds waiting patiently at an end of season meet

The view from Sun Rising that I had so much admired those few months before was now beginning to help bring the jigsaw of Warwickshire life together in a way that was quite fascinating. The vast patchwork of farms that I saw below me on that first evening demonstrated to me how important our way of life is. This was and is today a wonderful example of how hunting fits completely naturally into the lives of those living and working in the countryside.

Across the Irish Sea and Back

With the Heythrop on one side of the Warwickshire country in the latter days of Captain Wallace, and the Bicester and Warden Hill on the other side with the young Captain Farquhar at the helm, all of us at the Warwickshire had to look sharp. The North Warwickshire were close by with their young team of lady masters under Captain Arkwright's guidance and we must not forget the Pytchley, who at the time were firmly in the hands of the Saunders family and were also in the business of producing top class results. There was no doubt we were in the thick of it and had a lot to live up to. However I don't think we did too badly and pretty well held our own. At this time I was becoming increasingly aware of standards and how important they were. They had been drummed into me since my youth, and I now understood that as we were surrounded by the big guns it demonstrated to me how much these values really mattered. Why? It was because all the packs around us and that includes the Warwickshire itself were run by the top class men and women of that time, either in the mastership or in the kennels, and this rubbed off on me.

Both Clarence Webster and Stephen Lambert had their own distinctive ways of hunting hounds and were equally successful at putting the Warwickshire foxes under some sort of pressure. What I don't think both men realised was just how influential they were being and how much this particular Barclay was soaking up from the whole experience. I felt like an all absorbing sponge not only trying to take in their ways, but also those of the next door establishments. From it came the ambition to carve one's own route, not only as a master but also hunting hounds. Clarence's hounds clearly adored him. His cheerful whistle and smiling face was enough to brighten up the dullest of days, and I am sure it had the desired effect on them as much as it did me and many others. He also had a pedigree in the hunting world rather longer than mine, which helped considerably.

The arrangement of two people hunting the same pack of hounds is never easy and unfortunately this came to an end after a while. Clarence retired and Stephen went on to hunt the Heythrop. However in my time with them the fox sense that my father had inadvertently taught me came further and further into play. What an animal. The respect that I learnt to give them came from those early days of watching them. It was either when they were being hunted or in the lazy days of summer when it was their turn to teach their young about hunting which was the most fascinating. Anyone who says the true hunting man does not have the greatest respect for his quarry, is talking nonsense.

Warwickshire was made for hunting. In those days which were really not that long ago, there was a significant amount of grass still left and although the large part of it was very heavy, the playing field provided for us was one hell of a place to learn the trade. It was well foxed and there weren't the restrictions there are today. No M40 slicing through the middle and not the heavy traffic making its way north to south and east to west like it does now. I don't think we realised just how lucky we were. Although the country was open and good sport could be shown in all parts, my particular favourite was the piece between Shipston-on-Stour down to the Heythrop borders at Moreton-in-Marsh. Coverts like Golden Cross, Oldborough, Blakemore, Aston Hale and more, fitted completely naturally into the landscape of the county. It is also important to remember the farmers who I mentioned in a previous chapter and whose guests we were and still are throughout each season. They are the ones who make up the rich pattern of any hunting country. Many good days were spent crossing the Fosse and excursions made up into the Heythrop country and sometimes further into North Cotswold territory were especially rewarding. It was where hounds could get on and do what they knew best and that was to hunt. No wonder that the great sporting artist Lionel Edwards took to this part of the world when he painted the hunted fox and the Warwickshire hounds coming away from that wonderful covert Dunsdon which stands proudly up on the bank between Moreton-in-Marsh and Toddenham village.

With the experience I was so fortunate to have acquired I was soon on my way to Ireland and the North Tipperary in a battered old farm van which, if I hadn't snaffled it up from my father, would shortly have ended up on the scrap heap. It nearly did so anyway as not long into our journey to the boat at Fishguard the gearbox fell through the floor, conveniently in the middle of the Heythrop country so help was not too far away. Nevertheless we eventually arrived at Dromineer on the banks of Loch Derg and the River Shannon and set up base in a rather damp flat above the stables at Kiltelagh, home of the Joint Masters of the North Tipps, Colonel and Mrs Dean. The next few months were certainly different and a considerable amount of knowledge was added to my Warwickshire experiences. The country that surrounded us was some of the most beautiful anywhere in the world. It was all grass with wonderful patches of gorse on the hillsides that were full of foxes. The kennels however were another matter. I had been used to five yards, concrete beds and yes, running water. The North Tipps Kennels were not quite on this scale - one muddy old yard and a nissen hut for a lodge with an old wooden bed. Running water was easily available although sadly not from a tap, but from the River Shannon which flowed a hundred yards away from the kennels. Twenty couple of hounds were resident and seemed remarkably happy. I had no choice but to get on with the job and make the most of it, no time for grumbling. Life here was unique and the few months I spent with the North Tipps were ones I shall never forget. They taught me just how spoilt I had been. Hunting is not all about large establishments with kennels full of staff undertaking every duty, it is the small two day a week packs who make up the majority both in Britain and Ireland and at times struggle to survive.

One of my main memories of this part of Ireland was that we seldom saw the sun. Rain came almost every day and from the moment my old dog and I arrived, to the time for us to return to England a few months later, we got absolutely soaked on most days. Keeping fit was not a problem though, as hauling water two buckets at a time from the river up the hill to fill the kennel troughs ensured a degree of strength in my upper arms that I never knew I had. Excursions to the Limerick, Tipperary and Duhallow Kennels were made during that summer. My days in Ireland were hard but they opened my eyes to the real world. However before long Warwickshire called again and I was to return to England to start work for the late Denny Green. What an adventure that was.

New Challenges

The time had now come to gain further agricultural experience. I had learned a fair bit about farming at home, but as Agricultural College loomed up on me, I wanted more practical knowledge so back to Warwickshire it was, to work for the legendary Denny Green. This was the beginning of more new and fulfilling challenges, however before we start, a few words are necessary about the man himself. He was without doubt a one off, the like of which we shall never see again. A countryman through and through who farmed in the heart of the Warwickshire country, Denny was someone who was totally dedicated, in his own single minded way, to the fortunes of farming and hunting. Perhaps one could be bold enough to say from experience that patience was not his strongest point. Everything had to be done at double quick speed and if you couldn't milk the house cow, feed the bullocks, lamb a ewe and cook the breakfast all at the same time, you weren't a lot of good. Dadglow possessed a flock of breeding ewes that were very important to Denny and as soon as hunting had finished lambing would get underway. It was virtually an all grass farm which was laid out for the sport and as a result life was never dull when the hounds came there to draw. Foxes would be flying in all directions, the fences would be tackled, and great fun would be had by all. He will be hugely missed and I am sure that all those who are fortunate enough to either live in Warwickshire or hunt with the Warwickshire hounds will feel his presence for many years to come.

I arrived at Dadglow on a Sunday afternoon in the middle of October. Denny, I was told, was at a party up the road and I should return the next morning, if my memory serves me correctly, at six thirty. I turned up as instructed but there was no sign of my new boss. This I thought was unusual, as he had a reputation for starting early, especially on a hunting morning, but a little later I found out the reason why. The party in the village had been serving alcohol, namely whisky and the boss who was normally someone who refrained from partaking in such refreshment, on his occasion had succumbed and the said drink had got the better of him. There was not going to be any hunting at Tadmarton for Mr Green this day that was for certain, or farming either. So after an aborted start, normal routine was resumed which meant looking sharp and no time to sit on one's backside. On one occasion though I did feel that he had taken all leave of his senses, as he left for hunting without giving me

any orders for the day except to light and watch the fire. So that is exactly what I did. The fire was lit, and the rest of the afternoon was spent keeping an eye on it as well as watching the racing and reading the newspaper, that was until a certain Mr Green walked in. I will leave his reaction to your imagination!

This was a time when there was no resident Mrs Green. Her place in the marital bed apparently having been taken by a fox, who when not asleep would awaken Mr Green by chewing his ears. Some mornings when I arrived for work, she would come flying down the stairs through the door and out into the yard. It is, I believe, true to say that at certain times in their marriage, the present Mrs Green, may have had to share the space with another one of the vulpine species. History does not go as far as to tell us whether she experienced her ears being chewed, I am sure she would be delighted to let anybody know who is brave enough to ask.

As well as being a busy livestock farmer, Denny had a great reputation for bringing on young horses and the yard was normally full of them in all shapes and sizes. This particular Barclay was not quite the weight he is now and as a result seemed to be put up on some of those whose nature, let's say, was not necessarily placid. Some hairy trips took place, jumping large fences whilst totally out of control was not uncommon, quite an eye opener for a plough country lad. However, I survived the year and when it came round to spring was still in a fit state for lambing, although quite how I am not sure. Now was the time for much work to be achieved to accomplish all that had been put back by the hunting. Top dressing, chain harrowing and rolling all took place and most importantly we built a new lambing shed, acquiring telegraph poles and corrugated sheets from every part of the county. This allowed Denny to expand his flock size considerably. The sheep were very important to him and his ability to lamb a ewe in difficulty was a good lesson for anybody who was developing an interest in livestock.

Summer came and went, haymaking and harvest, and then a new adventure. I was to attend the Hertfordshire College of Agriculture at St Albans. However a few days before I left, one of the highlights of my life was to take place. I was allowed to hunt the Puckeridge Hounds for the first time. This was not at Brent Pelham as had been the case for the rest of the family on reaching the age of 21, but at a place called Hadham Lodge near Bishops Stortford which belonged to Frank and Tiggy Harvey. This I have to say was partly my choice as they owned a wonderfully thick covert called Bloodhounds, pronounced Bluddens, which was normally full of foxes. It was beautifully laid out, about sixty acres in all with mown rides as they are at Badminton and large areas of impenetrable bramble bushes - just the challenge for which I was ready and looking forward. The day dawned misty with a heavy dew and nerves that were somewhat edgy. Ron Quarmby was whipping into me and inevitably Father was keeping a watchful eye on proceedings. We drew High Wood first down into the main covert and just as I put them in, he came to me and said very quietly: "I told you to draw this first to settle everything down, you won't find here but watch your old hounds, they will drift across into the main covert and up into the brambles where they have found countless times before." Of course he was dead right, that is exactly what they did. A wonderful piece of advice, which allowed them to do their bit in a totally natural way, without being hindered by me. They soon got going and for the next two and a half hours his dog hounds hunted with a lovely cry before finally catching a fox in full view of none other than Jim Meads. What a morning it had been and in just a few hours one that had taught me so much more about the foxhound and how they should be handled.

So it was off to college. My time with Denny had been very well spent and I shall never forget many of the things that we got up to, all of which stood me in good stead for a future in both farming and hunting. The College was not that far from Brent Pelham, perhaps forty miles or so, however the Puckeridge country came down to join the Enfield Chace borders much closer than that. It was inevitable that hunting was going to carry on in my life, although it probably should not have done if I was going to be a highly successful student. Instead between lectures and learning how to milk the cows, my father continued to allow me to hunt the Puckeridge Hounds in all the unfashionable bits of country nearest to London. This was the greatest fun in itself and I was able to show His Grace the Duke of Beaufort, when he visited to judge the Puppy Show, my little bit of urban country. I believe he thought I must have been quite mad.

Whilst at college I was also lucky enough to be given the opportunity to hunt the West Lodge Harehounds, another wonderful experience which I enjoyed tremendously, for which I have the late Jack Powell Williams to thank. The Enfield Chace and the Vale of Aylesbury were very close by so inevitably as much hunting as was possible took place in between lectures. All this stood me in good stead for what was to be my next move, the Heythrop.

Further Learning of the Ropes

My next stop was the Heythrop. This all came about as a result of a visit by Stephen Lambert to my father after he had been involved in a serious car crash. He had made us aware a week or two before that he had some plans he wanted to discuss with us which just might help me with my future. Having already been with him at the Warwickshire he had been thinking that I could be of assistance to him on his recent move to be a Joint Master and hunt the Heythrop. Again I needed to prove my worth and as I was still hunting hounds and looking after what we described as the "London country", a meet was arranged at Wadesmill Park. This is just off the busy A10 that runs from London to Cambridge. Planning hunting in this part of the world was a very good test for anybody let alone someone not long since left college. This was just the challenge I needed to show Mr Lambert what I could do and how very keen I was to follow in my father's footsteps. A job at the Heythrop would give me the required experience.

Between the meet and the dual carriageway was a large Convent called Poles Park which now happens to be a well known hotel named Hanbury Manor after Sampson Hanbury, one of the early Masters of the Puckeridge. To ensure a reasonable morning could be put together it was important for there to be good communication between ourselves at the Puckeridge Hunt and those at the Convent. So, one afternoon before Mr Lambert's intended visit, off I went and with no appointments made just managed to pluck up enough courage to make the all important visit. Arriving at the rather large front door, I introduced myself to the first available nun I noticed coming in from the garden. What a nerve racking experience, however I said I was James Barclay from the Puckeridge Hunt and politely asked if it was possible to meet the Mother Superior. I was duly taken down miles of corridors to her office where I was given a chair and a cup of tea and made to feel most welcome. Mother Superior then proceeded to ask in a most courteous manner, what she could do to help. I explained that we were hoping to meet at the next door farm and could we possibly draw their Park with the obvious important considerations to them. Please remember this was one of my first experiences of this kind. I had been used to visiting the great sporting farmers that Hertfordshire and Warwickshire produced and now I was asking the Mother Superior if we could hunt the land around her Convent. Well the smile said it all. In a soft Irish accent, she pronounced that she would only be too pleased for us to do so and how she held some wonderful memories of hunting in Ireland as a child.

Well if that wasn't good enough for Mr Lambert, what was? I hoped that I hadn't lost any of the tact both he and my father had drummed into me, so when we were discussing this potential further employment he had in mind, I let him know exactly what had actually been done to provide him with his morning with the Puckeridge Hounds. Still, he felt it was important for him to observe more closely how I performed on the day, before making a final decision. This was interesting as it was not me that was going to be hunting the Heythrop

Hounds, that was for certain. I thought I was just going to be the boy of no consequence, as I become known from my time in Warwickshire. Never mind, the following morning whilst it was still dark we headed down the A10 as if we were going straight into the northern part of the Capital. The orange glow of London's lights were there right in front of us and I think my potential new boss might have wondered for a moment where the hell I was taking him. However, not many miles short of the metropolis, we turned off at a wonderfully named pub, the Sow and Pigs at Thundridge, and went down the side of the Convent to the Meet at Wadesmill Park. Here we were met by the charming Hodge family who farmed there and could not have been more supportive. Putting a morning's hunting together between a dual carriageway, a gravel pit, a waste disposal site, a Convent as well as another main road or two was interesting to say the least, still we achieved our aim. This was largely due to the local backing that we received but especially from two brothers whose enthusiasm for the chase stood out. They were Derek and John Jones. Derek farmed at Chapmore End near Hertford, and was always a great help to us. John had left the family home to end up as Head Keeper to Lord Dulverton in the Heythrop country. Here he was renowned for being hugely sympathetic, keeping both foxes and pheasants. His experiments were well worth taking note of then and are still hugely beneficial now. Although John was not out on this occasion he very often came up from Batsford to meets in this part of the world and the local farmers and keepers were always pleased to see him.

Well, to hunt a pack of hounds in the best of hunting countries in front of a field full of critics is one thing but to do so in front of the new Master and Huntsman of the Heythrop was even more daunting I thought, especially when you are trying to hunt a fox round the edge of a rubbish tip just north of London. I can't have done it too badly though as I was given the job and shortly found myself in Chipping Norton. This was just two years after Captain Wallace had left for Exmoor, so it really was like going from the frying pan into the fire as I knew how high people's expectations there were. This was a country that had ticked like clockwork for the last twenty-seven years. Fences, gates, bridges and fox coverts were all beautifully maintained and hounds had been bred to the highest degree both in their looks and their ability to hunt. Although our standards at Brent Pelham were just as high, it was still daunting to set foot on a place like this. I can assure you there was a fair amount of fear and trepidation on that Sunday afternoon in the middle of October 1980.

The first person I needed to call on was Tony Collins who had whipped in to the Captain and had hunted the hounds since his departure. From the beginning of the season of 1980/81 Stephen hunted the bitches and Tony the dog hounds. It was three o'clock when I arrived at his back door with a brace of pheasants that my father had asked me to give him with his compliments. That was my first mistake. I was all but ordered from the door and was only allowed in when I promised to take them away. "They are vermin", Tony pronounced, "Never

 bring anything like that here again otherwise we will soon fall out!" That was a good start, but things soon improved and it was a pleasure to observe the wonderful rapport Tony had with his hounds. They were treated as if they were his family and their welfare was of paramount importance to him.

From then on and for the next two seasons we had many happy days and, like Warwickshire, I

The Heythrop Hounds ready for boxing up

could not have been at a better place to learn the trade. Life spent just over the border was made all the more interesting when the Heythrop hounds ran into Warwickshire country and many times I was on hand to see the Warwickshire hounds hunted by Tony Collin's former Whipper-In, Anthony Adams, coming in from the opposite direction. Occasionally the inevitable would happen and they would join up and then sparks would soon start to fly.

Now more about my job description. Basically, it was varied. I started as the number two assistant to Geoff Tomlin, the highly regarded fencing man for whom I developed a huge respect and learnt so much from him. Geoff was a true countryman who quietly got on with his job in a way that astounded me. I spent many an hour with him and his knowledge of the Heythrop country was phenomenal. He knew each area of the country like the back of his hand and worked at a pace which ensured all the daily tasks were undertaken before returning home. There was absolutely no point in flying from one job to another. There was always a structured plan, he prioritised what needed to be done and either repaired or improved the access points for the future. This was more than likely over a cup of tea, a sandwich or just a fag. In those first few days I remember thinking that our work was exasperatingly slow, but how wrong I was, Geoff knew exactly what he was doing and his popularity amongst the farmers of the Heythrop country said it all. Whilst helping him, I was also seconded into working closely with Stephen over the organisation of the hunting day which as we know is absolutely vital, but as we are also aware, it is not only what goes into the before, it is the afterwards which is so key to a Hunt's success. Please is one thing, but not to say thank you was and still is a criminal offence in our eyes. We had no right whatsoever to ride roughshod over anybody then, and we certainly don't now.

Learning Diplomacy

I probably learnt more about running a country at this time than any other and it certainly stood me in good stead for the future. When I look back at those early days of collecting flesh in Warwickshire for Clarence or fencing in the Heythrop country with Geoff, it makes me realise just how important it is to run a Hunt properly and efficiently. Firstly though, let us imagine the scene. Mondays would produce fields of around one hundred, Wednesdays, anywhere between two hundred and two hundred and fifty. Fridays were the smaller days of about fifty to eighty and Saturdays, between two and three hundred, with the largest field I ever remember of three hundred and twenty. There were even weeks during the regular season when we hunted every day bar Sunday, which of course we had already done, all through cubhunting. In all my time at the Heythrop I only hunted once on a horse, being on foot/in a car, meant I was a good deal more use to Stephen. I was in a much better place to react quickly to problems and with help from the locals to work out which farmers Stephen and I should visit after hunting, also I could be there to help Geoff as and when required. When I explained in past chapters about being at the sharp end, I certainly was here and the reason why was soon to become clear.

The Mondays and a large part of the Fridays were spent between Banbury and Chipping Norton and were looked after by Stephen's Joint Master Oliver Langdale. The Wednesday and Saturday country was west and south west of Chipping Norton to Moreton-in-Marsh, Stow-on-the-Wold, and to Bourton-on-the-Water and beyond. The rest of the Friday country took in the land from Chipping Norton down towards Oxford, Burford, and over the A40 towards Cirencester. Although not the largest of hunting countries every bit of it was huntable. The reasons why at that time the Heythrop enjoyed almost unlimited access was because there had been exceptionally good farmer relations for a good many years, little shooting and in Captain Wallace's era he had encouraged those subscribers with city wealth behind them to buy land. Not so easily done today.

The Heythrop hacking home from Swell Wold

Despite the Captain convincing those Ladies and Gentlemen to purchase farms that would be useful to the hunt, a tremendous amount of effort had been spent to ensure those who did not possess the same deep interest in the sport as ourselves were always looked after properly. I think, if my memory serves me correctly, there was only one farm where access was denied and it was during my time with the Warwickshire that we happened to get on it. Not only that, it also happened to be the day when Stephen Lambert had kindly invited my Father to bring the Puckeridge Hounds to hunt the Warwickshire country. We met at Sutton-under-Brailes where Miss Boultbee Brooks, a former Master, kindly entertained us. After a busy morning around Traitors Ford, hounds got away well from Long Compton Coombes and ran as hard as they could clean into the Heythrop country, running into Over Norton Park and on almost into the back streets of Chipping Norton. When we got to the Park, the Puckeridge Hunt Supporters were seen hauling the hounds over the rather high wall which the fox had jumped up onto and ran for some yards before leaping off into unforgiving territory. Not knowing it was the only place where the Heythrop were not allowed we carried on until we could go no further. My Father, realising the Heythrop Kennels were just down the road, then made the swift decision that we should take the hounds there and everything should be sorted out before returning to Hertfordshire. On arrival, Tony Collins appeared in a rather shocked state, and made the comment that "All his adjoining packs enjoyed hunting in the Heythrop country and now the Puckeridge had to come all the way from b.......... Hertfordshire to do the same." Approximately twenty five years later the unwelcoming farmer rang me and asked if I had a Lincoln Red Bull for sale to cross with his South Devons and luckily the story was recalled with some amusement.

After hunting the work had to be put in to ensure all was well. It is important to remember that our fields were some of the largest anywhere so it was absolutely vital that we kept on top of the job. It is also interesting to note that at that time warning cards were still only sent out to keepers or earth stoppers to request they either night stop or put to in the morning. It was felt at that time that the farming community always knew when we were in the vicinity by checking the local paper where the meets were published weekly. On our evening visits we frequently would not get back to the Kennels till gone nine with more than likely a belly full of fruit cake and a certain amount of whisky and milk, just enough of course to line the stomach. It was important to know when to act swiftly and there was one such occasion that proves this point. The bitches were running hard out on the North Cotswold borders, when they suddenly changed direction and went back straight through the Waverton Stud, where there was a considerable number of rather valuable thoroughbred brood mares out in paddocks around the house. These were owned by Sir Jocelyn Hambro and as soon as we knew what had happened, a call was made to the Stud Groom. Although obviously concerned about the arrival of the Heythrop hounds from afar, he was very good about it, but felt it would be wise to pay a visit to the Boss. So at the end of the day I loaded up my battered old, open backed Land Rover with Stephen and Valerie Wills, his Joint Master. Mrs Wills was wedged in between us like a sardine in a can and did not look overly comfortable with her head just peering over the dashboard, however off we set. In the back were my scruffy old terrier and lurcher, so imagine the scene. After proceeding through lots of electric gates we found our way to the front door where Sir Jocelyn was waiting for us looking rather harassed. Not so much possibly about the hounds turning up on his doorstep but the sight of what was coming down the drive. Anyway all turned out well and the entourage was invited in and forgiven.

It was absolutely extraordinary. Hunting, farming and breeding racehorses in that part of the world as in many places is inextricably linked, but to think we could gallop two hundred plus horses across their land and were made most welcome afterwards, really left its mark on me. So many of those whom we hunted over were proper hard working mixed farmers, they were the absolute salt of the earth. I will always be grateful to them for what they taught me. More than a year at Agricultural College ever did. The knowledge they imparted was invaluable and became extremely useful as farming was later to become an increasingly important part of my life.

The Heythrop was a big team. With four in the kennels, five in the stables, plus a terrierman and fencer, it was a force to be reckoned with. Roger Bigland was Terrierman, and amongst other things in charge of stopping. However, his work during the early spring to my mind was vital. The contribution to the environment through covert maintenance was where we put an immense amount back into the land we hunted. Coverts which were drawn four or five days a year would be laid and made warm and dry for every conceivable wild animal or bird to take advantage of throughout the year and it was only on those few occasions when they would they be disturbed. Here the word balance came to the fore and demonstrated why Great Britain was lucky enough to possess the most healthy fox population anywhere in Europe and across the world. This was also the time of year for the hedge laying and the best rebuilt stone wall competitions would be judged, again showing an all round commitment. So with Geoff Tomlin either re-fencing or improving access, Roger carrying out his work in the country as well as what was going on at the Kennels and the breeding of a first class pack of hounds, what better place could I have had to work? It was then and only then I took on board just how important hunting's contribution to the countryside was and still is today.

One day Stephen asked if I would go down to Moreton-in-Marsh station and see if I could locate someone I could talk to with regards to setting up a better understanding between the railways and the Hunt. This had been undertaken by the late Michael Downes in the Captain's day but had now lapsed and the situation needed addressing. A visit to the signal box paid dividends and within no time an arrangement was made that really worked not only for us, but for the Warwickshire and the North Cotswold too. As a result a number of train drivers and signalmen became good friends of the Hunt and with many individuals. It is only in recent years that I have lost contact with them as they have now all retired. We were able to thank them at the earth stoppers dinner at Bourton-on-the-Water on an evening in April 1983, when fourteen signalmen, fourteen drivers and their two bosses arrived in a bus from Worcester. If my memory serves me correctly there was not a drop of alcohol left in the place and every pot plant off the tables disappeared back to Worcester, as they said they would need them to keep their wives happy. It was on that occasion that the father of Kevin Connolly, the BBC's reporter, told me to be at Moreton Station for 9.15 on Tuesday morning as I was to drive the train to Oxford. What a memorable day, particularly when we got to Oxford and he took me down to the Station Hotel where a group of drivers was waiting to give me breakfast. They had picked up that I was off to pastures new in a week or two and they wanted to say thank you for including them in the workings of the Heythrop Hunt. That is something which will always be in my memory of great days past, but more importantly I will always remember they were the ones who, with good humour, never once faltered from making our arrangements work. They were a cracking group of chaps to work with and a privilege to know.

So, as 1st May came, it was back across to the Eastern Counties to hunt the Essex and Suffolk and the many more new experiences I was to face.

A Brief Look at the Important Responsibilities of Mastership

It was 1st May 1983 when I was appointed to hunt the Essex and Suffolk Hounds, with the well known Suffolk agriculturalist George Paul and his wife Mary as my Joint Masters. Mastership had finally come my way but now was the time more than ever to put into practice everything I had learnt over the previous seven plus years. I had been incredibly fortunate in the education I had received and I sure as hell wasn't going to let down those who had made it all possible. However, before we delve deeply into my four seasons there, I thought it would be an appropriate time to write a bit about what I have learnt of the role of Masters and the many different challenges that face them today. The responsibilities of sound management are crucial, and with the spotlight being permanently upon us it is hugely satisfying that there are so many people who are prepared to give of their valuable time, making sure hunting has a solid future. This in itself says a lot about our sport, as running a hunt is a complex business at any time but especially during the present climate. We must never forget though that goodwill is not only the driving force behind our survival, it is the glue that keeps it together and should never be neglected or over looked. Although our hunts cannot operate without finance, this is the number one rule that needs adhering to throughout a Mastership. It will have huge benefits all round.

Before we get going, let us just cast back to the year of 1983 and have a look at where hunting was then. Over all it would appear from the outside we were in good shape, however there were problems bubbling beneath the surface which as we know later came to haunt us. Politically we were in a fairly settled time, with a Labour Government looking as though they would, in the words of the late Baroness Thatcher, "never gain power again". This was a most unfortunate thing to say as it certainly came back to bite us on the backside. We were though in a very different place to where we are now, but despite all the efforts from the opposition and the continued battering hunting has taken, it is still here, in its many different forms, and we should be extremely proud of the fact. This is very largely due to the resilience of countrymen and women up and down the land and also those who have been responsible for running their Hunts and steering many of them through what from 2005 have been extremely tough times.

During the early eighties it became quite clear that certain Labour politicians were not going to give up on achieving their long term goal. Part of their plan was to do everything they could to encourage County Councils to ban hunting on their land. It did not worry them in the slightest that they were taking the right of the tenant to decide whether they could allow hunting to take place or not clean away. This was a draconian measure to say the least. It was when hunting was banned in the London Borough of Islington that we knew the lengths they were going to, but they continued to build on their successes and as we know only too well, dealt what they thought was the final blow in February 2005. Although we can always say we could have done more, we put up one hell of a fight, that was for sure, but listening to reason certainly was not on their agenda. None of us were going to take it lying down and with a huge amount of innovation we rose again from the ashes and although it looks as if we are not going to see any reversal of the act in the near future, we still have everything to play for. Now, as the new season begins, it is not the time to be down hearted, it is the time to celebrate what we do have and to go out there and inspire others in a way that will make them realise that hunting in its truest form needs to be brought back and for common sense to prevail. This is the time more than ever, as old Masters bow out, to give our new incumbents all the support they need to make a success of running the job. They are the sport's future, and it is up to us who have been there before to help them be the success they deserve.

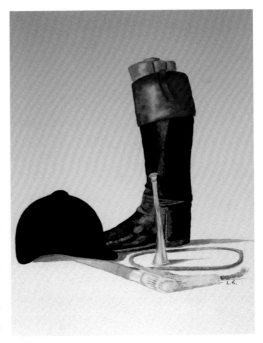

Without good leadership and experienced professionals still there to give us a lead across country we certainly would not be where we are today. We more than likely would have sunk without trace, so whilst it is easy to criticise those who are in charge or who hunt the hounds we should always find the time to listen to them. It is they who put themselves on the line on our behalf. I know only too well having been there that fair criticism is fine, but there are lorry loads of it out there that isn't and pacifying everyone can waste crucial time when many important issues need addressing. Some of our old guard are notoriously bad at this and in blunt terms, need to know when to shut up.

If you now have MFH after your name, remember whilst it may be very rewarding to have the title of Master of Foxhounds, it also can mean, More Fool He or Her. Primarily it is most important for you to enjoy it, for not doing so will bring great despondency to you and your family. Then there is always the danger when things go wrong, which inevitably they will at some point, that alcohol will be consumed and fags smoked. This can equally be the case when it is all going along nicely as some Masters know only too well. Whilst there are very heavy responsibilities on Masters up and down the country we have to demonstrate to the population as a whole that we are a decent and caring section of society. One foot wrong with nothing done about it leads to a mountain of problems but more about that later.

For a new Master life after 1st May is never going to be the same again, starting with constant phone calls, more than likely just at the time you are about to eat your evening meal. But having taken on this great responsibility it cannot be ignored, even though your wife or husband will soon be nagging you to take the b...... phone off the hook. It is always wise to try and resist that pressure if you can, especially after hunting as there may well be a farmer trying to contact you to discuss key issues that have occurred during the day. Of course there are times that all Masters need to relax but that is what night time and a bed is for. Whilst at the sharp end, your Hunt is very much under your watch and you can never completely take time out unless there is someone to cover for you. As you progress through the summer, the number one priority must be to get out there and visit every farmer over whose land you are likely to cross during the coming season. Depending on your country this often has to be undertaken within a very narrow window of opportunity as by the time they have finished lambing you can bet your life time will fly and harvest will soon be upon them. However keen your farmers are, they definitely won't want to see you when delivering a lamb or when covered in dust having just come down from the combine to meet you. Timing is of great importance, as is the way you present yourself to them. There is no hard and fast rule, but just be normal and if there have been problems in the past that they want to hit you with, don't argue, be humble and ensure they get a clear message that you want to put things right. This can be easier said than done but you will develop a knack for it, just don't rush yourself or them as that will certainly backfire.

During your summer visits it may be wise to have a map with you, although I personally did not do this, preferring to go to a point where you can see various landmarks, such as church towers and spires, radio masts, grain silos etc. and try and imagine all the farmers you have seen that feed back to those points. Their boundaries will then become clear in your mind and you will gain great satisfaction from this when asked by one of your subscribers whose land you are on. A map on the hunting day does not look very professional, and can add to unnecessary clobber in your hunting coat but after a day's hunting I took a huge amount of pleasure in examining them to see exactly where we had been that day. Before you visit also try to gain as much information as you can as this will undoubtedly help you as you progress round what I happen to call, your parish. This term is not used in a light hearted way, it is because interestingly enough Masters on their travels round can after a while be looked upon not in a dissimilar way to that of the local rector, who knows everyone and when to call. It is then that you very soon pick up when things aren't just quite as they should be. This in the rector's case will normally be over a cup of tea and should be of course for an MFH but it has been known, just occasionally, for it to be something of a stronger nature. If it is suspected that this could occur then make sure somebody is with you to drive you home. Taking your Huntsman with you is never a bad idea, as he will have great knowledge of the country, not only who is who but where they have run in previous seasons. This is a very good time for both Master and Huntsman to build up respect for each other as communication between the two of you on a hunting day is vital for success. Keeping notes from your visits will undoubtedly help you, even if it is only a brief description of the characters you have met. There will always be an occasion when you meet someone out of context and they will know you, and will expect you to know them. The old saying "More people know Tom Fool than Tom Fool knows" comes to mind at this time.

So, as summer progresses you should have started to get to know your country, and if you are fortunate enough to have been given the dual responsibility of huntsman, your hounds. It will be a busy part of your life and a steep learning curve as there is a great deal to take on board. If you are also employed elsewhere be prepared, as you will find running a hunt takes up an enormous amount of time so please make sure you do not overstretch yourselves. The worst case scenario would be that nobody has told a farmer you might be in his area and you end up running there. It can lead to difficult situations and then you will need all the tact and diplomacy you can muster to extract yourselves out of the mire. Always be ready to act and act quickly. Leaving things to the next day, does not always work, strike whilst the iron is hot if you can as people want to see the person in charge. There are no hard and fast rules but nine times out of ten they will have respect for the person who turns up on the door step and explains the situation and if needs be, apologises. Running away is not an option. There will be other situations which undoubtedly will occur during the day and where immediate action is required. If we ignore those we ignore them at our peril, left overnight the incident can fester in the mind and so the transgression will appear to increase.

There will be many events throughout the year that are either run by the Hunt or the Supporters Club and it is important that at least one Master attends as those who run them like to see you there. It is an excellent

a priority during the summer, however there is no better way of learning it than from the back of a horse with a pack of hounds in front of you. So we got on with the job and over time I could see the hounds were really beginning to gel. I believe that because they had a naturally good cry it helped them run up together.

Towards the end of October I took a trip down to the West country, firstly to the North Cotswold as Roy Tatlow who was hunting them at the time said he had something that he hoped would be of use to me. This turned out to be two third season bitches, Lilac and Gaudy, both of whom proved to be cracking in their work. I will always be grateful to Roy for his support and generosity. My next port of call that day came as a result of a letter from Badminton. The Duke, who had always been so kind, offered me a good sized lemon and white bitch called Ticket. She had won the championship at Peterborough a year or two before and His Grace thought she could be of benefit which, like the other two I had just been given, she certainly was. More on this a little later as we are now coming up to the time of our two Opening Meets. The Suffolk side traditionally held theirs in Hadleigh Market Square and the Essex side was always at Horsley Cross, a pub on the A120 half way between Colchester and the Port of Harwich. The difference between the two pieces of country was most pronounced, with gently rolling hills behind the town of Hadleigh and Horsley Cross being stuck out in one of the flattest and most open parts of Essex imaginable. You would wonder where a fox would even lie, but make no mistake they were there. George always hunted them from Hadleigh and Horsley Cross was my responsibility with Joint Master Mary field mastering for me.

The name Jiggens is very well known in that part of Essex. John was Master with Rowley Hitchcock and what a pair they were. John hunted the hounds on his side of the country with Charlie White as his First Whipper In and Kennel Huntsman. The fun they had between them is well recorded. If legend is to be believed Charlie didn't only have the job of whipping in, he would be sent on well in front, not to get a view but to go to the nearest pub and ensure the Master's flask was swiftly refilled with that brown liquid for which most Huntsmen have a taste. His son Jack in due course joined me in the Mastership but before that was a very able amateur Whipper In. He was the one who would go well ahead and get a good view and did not, I may add, have the responsibility of refilling this particular Master's flask. His then wife Jane always had a large piece of beef on the table at the end of each day and with a loaf of bread, a pound of butter and extra roast potatoes, she was responsible for keeping this young bachelor Master free from starvation.

Whether it was Suffolk or Essex mattered not, it was a tremendous place to be to learn the true art of venery. Unlike the Heythrop Hounds the Essex and Suffolk had to draw wide to find their fox and once they had got going keeping with him was important for there were unlikely to have been many others in the area. On one occasion towards the end of November I observed a beautiful piece of houndwork and it was Ticket who performed it to absolute perfection. We were in the latter stages of a long old fashioned plough country hunt which had been quick slow, quick slow all the way. The fox had run up a deep furrow right to the embankment of the Colchester / Harwich road, and initially looking at it you would have thought he had the time to go straight over, as this particular road was normally fairly quiet at that time of day and was only really busy when the ferries were in. Be that as it may, I watched Ticket very carefully as she put her head down and for at least two hundred yards ran straight back down whence they had come. It was at that point one might have been forgiven for thinking it was either heel or that 'Charlie' had actually been headed, but she kept going, speaking occasionally until she came to a single large oak tree and this is where she crossed a large ditch. Then with her very distinctive voice she hit it off with renewed confidence and took the whole pack, now in full cry, across a large acreage of winter wheat. On they went for another half a mile before marking in a land drain. This had been a fascinating hunt to watch and taught me to make the time during a hunt to watch and observe everything that is going on around you. Sir Andrew Horsburgh-Porter once described in The Field a very good hunt with the Puckeridge when Father was hunting the hounds. They had run well into a field of clover off some heavy plough. Sir Andrew could not work out why on what was apparently clean ground they could only hunt slowly across it. My Grandfather who had been riding wide of them was asked at tea why this was the case. He told them he had observed a flock of starlings taking off from that very field as the fox had crossed it some ten minutes before. Starlings as everyone knows are very smelly and so would have disguised any scent of the fox. This again demonstrated the importance of accurate observation and the help it can be to a Huntsman on any day at any time. Quick decisions are vital but must be based on that one word, accuracy. Better at times to take just a little longer and ensure the right one is made, especially in a bad scenting plough country.

Playing with Fire!

In early December I received a call from Captain Wallace to say he was coming up to the Eastern Counties and would like to have a day in the car with us. Well, as you can imagine, this put the fear of God not only in me but all of us. He happened to choose a meet which was probably the most difficult one on the card and was sandwiched between two main roads with Colchester not far away either. We prepared ourselves as best we could and hoped that we had put enough country together to give our visitor from on high a reasonable day. Coats were cleaned to perfection, boots polished until you could see your face in them and sixteen and a half couple drawn out for him to inspect. With everything ready I was just about to sit down to my evening meal when the phone rang and the very distinctive voice announced it was "Ronnie Wallace here" and that he was unable to come in the morning because it was necessary for him to attend an important meeting in London. Well, there was a certain amount of relief I have to say, but I also believe it would have been very good for us if he had come as maybe we could have learnt a lot from him. Like many of his generation he was very supportive of us younger huntsmen and he kept a genuine interest in what we were all trying to achieve. As a result of this I was privileged for him to judge my last Essex and Suffolk Puppy Show in 1987. This was the day the young bitches coursed the kennel cat, Newman, round the field right in front of him. It was their normal party trick but was something we could quite well have done without on that occasion.

Hunting three days a week kept us busy all round and did not leave a great deal of time for me to open up new country. Looking after our farmers was an absolute priority but it was also vitally important that the area we were hunting at the Essex and Suffolk was increased. I was particularly keen to do this as it would help to take the pressure off where we were hunting regularly. I began by looking at the country and saw two parts

The Shotley Peninsula looking towards Felixstowe and Harwich Docks

with potential. To the north there was a nice area which adjoined the Easton Harriers which, although quite flat, was wild and had never been hunted by foxhounds. How enticing for this young and enthusiastic MFH. The Shotley peninsula was also worthy of further investigation. This is an area of land that sticks out into the North Sea, with the Stour estuary and Harwich on one side and the River Orwell and Felixstowe's massive container port on the other. It had been hunted a few times by the Sproughton Foot Beagles who then went on to amalgamate with the Colchester Garrison and become the Stour Valley Beagles. No mounted pack had ever been out on the peninsula before, so with all to play for in both places, nothing could possibly hold me back, could it?

Looking at a map in the MFHA office one day I observed that the Essex and Suffolk country was registered out to Aldeburgh on the coast and everything had been signed by Rowley Hitchcock and John Jiggens to back it up. This was just what I needed to know and off I went to prepare. A week or two later we were stopped by frost and this gave me the opportunity to make a start. I had been led to believe there was a great character in that part of the world called Alfred Jennings. He farmed a considerable acreage at Winston Green near Debenham and so was the key to opening up all the land around him. Sure enough he was just as I had been told, and what a good friend he became. Word soon got around about our proposed plans but little did I realise that through my inexperience I was about to start playing with fire, actually a raging inferno, which took some damping down. I had ventured into territory where the Essex and Suffolk Hounds were not welcome, not by the farming community but by the Easton Harriers, who made it very plain that this was a non starter. We were seriously treading on some toes and action had to be taken quickly to try and resolve it. Perhaps I should have been a little more diplomatic with them to start with but I presumed, probably somewhat stupidly, that if I looked after the farmers in that part of the world as I had been taught at the Heythrop, then all would be well and we could work together quite happily. This was unfortunately not the case as we were in the only part of the whole of the UK where hare hunting had supremacy over foxhunting. What happened next became known as the Battle for Winston Green. This was so named because it was a key area for us but I had reckoned without the fury of Tony Harvey, long serving Master of the Harriers. He and I would sit in his Subaru truck and argue back and forward about our respective claims on the land. After long fruitless talks which went precisely nowhere, it was decided that arbitration was the only way left to go, so it was off to London to the British Field Sports Society Offices in Kennington Road. Lord Somerleyton and John Kirkpatrick represented the Masters of Harriers and Beagles Association and Ronnie Wallace and Anthony Hart the MFHA. Eventually, after a long afternoon a compromise was found and the go ahead given to hunt a sensibly sized area around Winston Green, although sadly this did not reach as far out as Aldeburgh. During the train journey back to East Anglia with Tony the misgivings we had for each other were put behind us and a great friendship began. This was despite the fact with gins in hand we got on the wrong train and led to us both getting home somewhat later than planned. Forgiveness I think if I remember correctly was found in the fact that we had worked hard all day for the interest of hunting in Suffolk.

I now had to concentrate not only on opening up this part of the country, but most crucially making sure that the farmers had the same amount of confidence in us as they did in Tony Harvey and the Easton Harriers. It was also important at this time to get to grips with what could be achieved on the Shotley peninsula. The challenges were just beginning but what a pleasure it was when our first meet at Winston Green was finally arranged for early February. A week or two before I was summoned to lunch with Alfred to discuss in detail the plans he envisaged for the day. Lunch here was a gastronomic affair and always ended up with a Walls Vienetta for pudding, a great favourite all round, which did nothing whatsoever for the waistline but showed what a character he was. Alfred, having been a shooting man all his life, had decided that hunting was by now far more important to him. Consequently he threw his weight behind the Essex and Suffolk and the Easton Harriers in a way which benefited hunting all round. This was hugely appreciated by all of us from both Hunts and we were assured if ever there was any discontent he was the first to help us sort it out.

So the scene was set. Every farmer had been visited and the draw planned to make the most of a day which we had all been looking forward to. A large crowd of inquisitive people turned up at the Meet to see what this Foxhunting game was all about. "Your Hounds are much bigger than ours" was one remark that amused me from an Easton supporter. Anyway, we got on with the job in hand, and on looking for some outliers around Alfred's hedgerows a fox appeared out of a thick brambly ditch and away our hounds went, as hard as they could possibly go, in a totally different direction to that we had planned. Running for forty minutes flat out into completely unknown territory was nerve racking to say the least. Even more so when we caught up with them as the fox had disappeared under an old shed in the middle of nowhere and I have to admit, I had no idea whose land we were on. Finding a hard track I trotted the hounds as quickly as I could back towards the road only to be met by a very red faced and angry farmer. Oh my God I thought, how the hell do I get out of this? All I could do was to apologise profusely and tell him that the fox we were hunting had gone to ground under the shed. "Fox?" he said. "Fox? You mean to say you are not the Norwich Staghounds?" I explained who we were and where we came from. On realising we were not who he thought we were he asked me if we would despatch the said animal as he had been losing no end of poultry. We duly obliged but not only was the hunted fox in residence, there were three more besides. Two of which were allowed to live another day and catastrophe was narrowly avoided. For the rest of the day the hounds did their absolute best and I was extremely proud of them. However it wasn't the only time the poor old things were mistaken for the Norwich Staghounds. This was not because they were seen misbehaving, it was because the Norwich Staghounds, who had been very much part of life in that part of Suffolk, used to turn up totally unannounced on one of their long straight hunts on a carted stag. This had more than likely been turned out somewhere way up in Norfolk and was making its way down to Shrublands Park near Ipswich where the hunt would come to an end. The stag would very often be left out there as he would have been difficult to recapture, thus avoiding his trip back and being turned out in the deer paddocks at the Kennels. It was a day which will last long in the many happy memories I have of hunting the Essex and Suffolk hounds.

Hunting the Shotley peninsula came next and whilst slightly more difficult to organise because of a very intensive shoot, we made a start which in time became easier. This was all a great experience for me, learning the ropes first hand and how to nurture and open up more country as required.

More country Opened and Meeting a Wife

Having worked hard at opening up the country, hunting on the Shotley peninsula eventually became a little easier although we were somewhat wedged in with it being approximately only four miles wide. We also had to contend with a very intensive shoot who decided rather unfairly that access should be completely denied. This was particularly difficult to swallow as there were hunting connections here which could, if they had wished, have made life very much easier. However those who farmed the peninsula could not have been kinder or more supportive. Hunting on early September mornings along the banks of the Orwell and Stour estuaries was quite something and memories of them are just as vivid as our trips out to Horsey Island. Although this was a part of the world which was not heaving with foxes, there were always enough to make it interesting and worthwhile. It was just a matter of getting to know where to look for them and despite the shoot trying to clear up even the last one, they failed to do so. This came down to the fact that their neighbours had a much better attitude

Roe Deer

to management of the species than they did. We were helped considerably in this direction by a top class butcher called Peter Hollingsworth. He and his family were well respected in the area and his enthusiasm for the chase and the love he held for the area was well known. This certainly made a difference to me and much less difficult than if I had been going in cold. It also had other benefits as being a single man at that particular time, I greatly valued a pack or two of his sausages to take home after hunting. All in all this had been another very worthwhile experience and it is extremely gratifying to see over thirty years later, despite all the challenges hunting has faced, the Essex and Suffolk Hounds are still welcome there.

At the previous year's Point-to-Point I was introduced to an Essex and Suffolk stalwart, Major Taylor, and his two daughters, Jill and Lucy. Jill worked in London and was then the non-hunting sister, whilst Lucy was a travelling cook and a most enthusiastic young subscriber. Several years later, when I had got to know Lucy somewhat better, she told me that when we met and I had shaken her hand, I looked straight over the top of her head, some 14 inches below mine, at somebody she was sure I would far rather have been talking to. I am not sure this was true, but be that as it may, it occurred to me that a cook was probably a person worth getting to know. After all it was very hard work hunting a pack of hounds and looking after myself as well. It is also important to remember that one hundred percent concentration is vital when you are hunting hounds, however the odd lapse is bound to occur, and so it was when my Joint Master Mary would send a certain girl on to the end of the covert we were about to draw. Flying past me going like a bat out of hell it could only have been one particular person, and I soon learnt that she happened to be a speed fiend and would go from nought to seventy in three seconds and that was just on her little mare Marnie. The pair of them had a habit of being right up beside our Field Master all day, whatever the pace.

International relations are very important in every walk of life and hunting is no different, so when a group of Frenchmen came over to pick up some hounds I decided a little help in entertaining them was required. I therefore plucked up courage and asked this young lady if she would be prepared to come over to have supper and converse with them in French. She duly obliged and charmed the Frenchmen and a certain English man in demonstrating almost fluently her enthusiasm for "La Chasse". The Frenchmen departed and still over thirty years later remind us both of the first time they were fortunate enough to meet Lucy. Her enthusiasm for the sport never waned but occasionally her lack of diplomacy got her on the wrong side of the Master. Towards the end of the season George and Mary Paul went visiting to Devon and Cornwall, on their annual pilgrimage with half the pack, leaving me to carry on at home but somewhat short of hounds. We were hunting with fourteen and a half couple up on our borders with the Suffolk when a roe buck leapt up right in front of them and away went two and a half couple of young ones. Lucy roared off in her normal way to stop them, accompanied by Richard Wilson, one of our best subscribers, eventually returning with broad smiles exclaiming that they had just "enjoyed the best hunt of the season!"

As our season drew to a close in Suffolk, George was still away with his hounds so it was left to me to finish up. Our last meet was held at the Layham Queen's Head and what a day we had. We covered a huge amount of country and never stopped running all day and I have to say I was very proud of the hounds. We finished up hacking back down the main street of Hadleigh at ten minutes to seven and just as we were about to turn down towards the Kennels, we saw approximately fifty motorcycles heading towards us. It was the Hells Angels. On approaching us they slowed right up, stopped and turned off their engines. The lead motorcyclist then took off his helmet and asked most politely what time did the pubs open in the town. "Seven o'clock" I said. What was to happen next really left its mark on me, as there we all stood for the next few minutes chatting away, with no antagonism whatsoever. That certainly taught me not to judge a book by its cover. Later that evening I was picked up and taken to an end of season dinner party and was seated next to Jill Taylor who soon was to become my Sister in Law. I am afraid I rather disgraced myself and quite how I was forgiven I shall never know. Throughout each course I was wide awake, probably banging on about what a good day we had and then between courses as the plates were cleared I went out like a light. My punishment was to be nudged hard in the ribs and from the other side of the table a severe glare.

Life went on happily and then the day came. Lucy and I were returning separately from the Easton Harriers country late one Friday evening when I stopped my car on a stretch of road very close to where the Battle for Winston Green had taken place. Plucking up the necessary courage I leapt into Lucy's car and asked her if she would marry me. Thankfully the answer was in the affirmative and so off I went contentedly back to my digs at the Kennels in order to be ready for our Point to Point the following day. However before I could even think about going racing, I had to go and ask the Major if I could marry his daughter. Bravely I asked the question, not expecting the swift reply "Which one?" At least this made me realise that I was dealing with a family which, amongst other things, had a certain sense of humour. We were not to be married until the next April though, so it was important to concentrate on the job in hand, hunting the Essex and Suffolk Hounds and looking after their country to the best of my ability.

Observations of the Hounds and some Public Relations

I had certainly taken much on board during my first couple of seasons but there was still a considerable amount to learn about handling hounds, both in the kennel and also, most importantly, hunting them. Foxhounds are a fascinating breed but as many of us in the business know, they do not take kindly to being mucked about, therefore it was with thanks for the good advice of Alex Ford, our then Kennel Huntsman, that the sound principles of kennel management started to fit into place. The hunting ability of the hounds which were already resident could not really be questioned. They had drive and cry and the old ones had the necessary fox sense which obviously helped, however there were areas where we needed to improve and if we were going to be successful, we really needed to concentrate on getting it right. One of the things that had been worrying me for some time came to a head on a day towards the end of the season. I still doubted myself and I was not sure if the problem lay with the hounds which had come from easier parts of the world than Suffolk, or if the way I was handling them, was to blame. In hindsight I feel it was more than likely a combination of a lack of experience on my part and a touch of laziness on theirs. However after a certain amount of observation we began to sort it out with no casualties.

What I suspected came to light when we were in the middle of what was turning out to be a nice hunt on a fair scent. The fox had run straight up a hedge behind the village of Monks Eleigh village and on reaching the

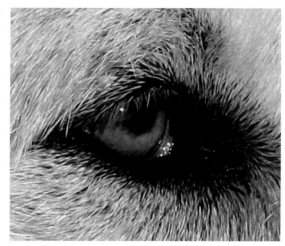

Observing

top of the hill turned away across a large field of winter wheat which if it had not been sprayed that day I suspect it had over the previous few days. They hunted well across into the middle and checked. Worryingly I noted that some of our more experienced draft hounds just stood there waiting for help whilst others were still trying. I watched patiently for a minute or two and then started to make my way towards them. I was about to intervene when I remembered seeing this happen with the Bicester just a few weeks earlier. I had been observing Ian Farquhar with a fag in his mouth standing there, dead still, letting his hounds sort the whole problem out for themselves and this they managed to do, without fault. So minus the cigarette, I left them to get on with it, it was fascinating to watch them and much more satisfying to know that my hounds had worked it out without my help. In future I would only step in as a last resort. Bit by bit the ones that had been trying gave the others the confidence and will they needed to succeed. After a little while they hit it off and away they went. This was rewarding to see, and although I should have picked up on this fault earlier in the season, I had been acting out of eagerness. Now though I had learnt better and from then on their teamwork started to develop. Hounds coming in from other kennels are likely to have their faults, however situations like this can teach not only a young Huntsman so much, but it helps the hounds to receive a positive message of what is expected out of them in a quiet and sensible way.

Jeremy Pembroke and Alfie Dyer had bred some outstanding hounds to hunt the plough and there were two litters by Exmoor Granby that stood out. I was fortunate enough to hunt Grafter, Grocer and Granger as well as Tonic, Tory, and Torchlight, and it was they along with Beaufort Ticket who helped save the day, as they did on numerous occasions. The rest of those two large litters hunted with George and I was very lucky to take them on when he retired at the end of the season. There was not one bad one amongst them and it was a privilege to hunt such high class hunting hounds.

The rest of the pack were moulding together and although not great beauties had attributes which were intriguing to watch both in and out of season. However something in the back of my mind was telling me that as well as engrossing myself in the hounds and looking after the country, I ought to be doing more to give people the opportunity to understand hunting and perhaps give them the chance to enjoy what I was experiencing. Therefore it turned out to be quite fortuitous when one Saturday morning out on bicycle exercise when I was least expecting it my PR skills were forced into action. We were on our normal routine just pedalling quietly away round the back of Holbecks Park when old Grocer noticed something a bit different. He nipped up the back drive and to his interest found a number of tents which at the time were being inhabited by a large number of scouts from Brixton, just waking up on their first morning in the beautiful Suffolk countryside. Within seconds he had disappeared into one of them for further investigation and as he reappeared, quite unfazed at being chased by screaming children, he decided to cock his leg up against a tent pole. Well, that did it. Within no time a very large, burly Cockney Scout Leader was there screaming at me to get my b........ dog away and what the hell did I think I was doing by letting him come into their area like that. Quick as a flash I asked Alex to hold the rest of the hounds for a minute whilst I put a damage limitation exercise into place. I shook the feller by the hand, apologised profusely and told him, as soon as we had put the hounds away, I would be back to see him. An hour later I was there, but how I was going to deal with the situation, I hadn't a clue, after all it was the first time anything like this had happened to me. I therefore thought it was best to play it safe and just apologise again and say no more, but as we were talking a cunning plan came to mind. Apologies are one thing but turning things around in our favour if at all possible are an absolute must, although that is sometimes easier said than done.

During a brief lull in proceedings I grasped the moment and said that whilst it was the most regrettable experience, I would be only too delighted to welcome him and his party to the Kennels that afternoon if they so wished. They could then enjoy the pleasures the hounds would give as well as the refreshments we would provide for them. The invitation was finally accepted with goodwill, so it was back to the Kennels sharpish to get organised for their 2pm arrival. The gap between town and country has been highlighted over many years, but the one between Brixton and ourselves was, you could say, quite immense, even back in 1984. Nevertheless this was a challenge that had to be faced and it was and still is our duty to ensure we do our very best to share with them the beauty of our countryside and where and how hunting fits in. A visit to Hadleigh for crisps, chocolate, and fizzy drinks was made, trestle tables dusted off and as the time approached for their arrival we found ourselves just about ready. As we had been rushing around I kept rehearsing to myself what I wanted to say and how I needed to put it across. After what was perhaps a jittery start, we got going and soon had them in amongst the hounds out on the lawn in front of the Kennels. We had brought some horses in so they could safely get up close to them and finally we took them into the grass yard to see the two litters of puppies that were ready for going out to walk. Hand washing facilities were provided and then every chocolate bar and fizzy drink was devoured in a matter of a few minutes. We made time to go round every child and every adult and talk to them about their visit, in the hope they had not only enjoyed it, but it had put their mind at rest. Thank God, it had done both in just the way we had hoped for and off they went, seemingly very happy with their experience. During the following week we kept seeing them and there was always a cheery wave for us as we cycled past. I often look back and wonder if what they saw that day over thirty years ago stayed with them. It was a good example to me that no opportunity should ever be lost to give young or old the chance of hearing our side of the story and in a way that makes them not only take notice but enjoy.

The Puppy Show, along with parades at Hadleigh and Tendring Shows, came and went without incident. So it was then on to hound exercise, which as we took to our horses was an increasingly important time for me to observe the hounds more and more closely. My predecessors used a technique called hare breaking which involved trotting out across large stubble fields and if a hare leapt up and the hounds took off they would chase after them with a lot of shouting and whip cracking. This was not for me and in my opinion could easily lead to a young hound losing its confidence. Quietness and kindness, with firm and fair discipline if required, was the way I had been taught and this worked much better for me. Shouting and bawling is unattractive and can very often lead to old hounds turning a totally deaf ear to what is expected of them. Frequently we would call on various households for refreshment, sometimes this led to visiting those non hunting farmers who we felt might be pleased to see the hounds out of season. Often this was totally unannounced but we were made welcome, quite why I don't know, but I presumed it was because the Essex and Suffolk have been part of rural Suffolk for very many years, and it was a place where enemies, thankfully, were few and far between. On our way back to the Kennels we would often trot down the High Street in Hadleigh to Mr Grimsey's shop where we would stop off for a few minutes. Mr Grimsey was one who gathered up the local information and gossip, so all would be divulged to the young MFH over a glass of whisky and milk. This was a great opportunity for the locals to pop in and have a quick word and certainly helped considerably in keeping ones finger on the pulse as to what was going on.

With Thanks to the Army and the RAF

Towards the latter part of August we made a start to our second season. There was no real hard and fast rule as to where we had to go, so this time, rather than heading out to sea and then following on into large acreages of sugar beet, we thought we would try something different - Friday Woods for the first three mornings. This was a large area of scrub and woodland which is owned by the Ministry of Defence and lies just at the back of the Military Corrective Training Centre at Colchester. I had thought hard about the pros and cons of where to go in those first few weeks and it was with the best interests of the hounds that this decision was taken. It was an area which is normally full of foxes and was a place where hounds could get themselves into the thick bits and hunt. We met at the Mersea Road Gate on the first morning with the mist coming up from the old Roman River, which set the scene for the start of another season. Moving off promptly, foxes were very soon appearing in every direction and it was not long before hounds were running in several different lots. I hoped that all things being equal this did not matter too much, as sooner or later they should come together as a single unit. Well on this particular day luck was on our side and after a good hour they settled on a strong fox that certainly did not resemble a cub. They kept on hunting until finally marking just below the old Colchester Garrison Beagle Kennels. This was where a large amount of poultry was kept and as you can imagine with such a plentiful supply foxes in the vicinity a considerable number of chickens and ducks had been lost to our vulpine friends over the summer months. With this in mind, I decided to account for the said animal. Well, what happened next caught all of us out. There were four very large foxes in the hole, all of which were

The Essex and Suffolk alongside RAF Wattisham perimeter fence

unusually early cubs and more than likely were from the same litter. Two of these were despatched with the other two being given their freedom. Some may say by doing so I was allowing them to continue dining rather well in the future. My hope was that this would give them a bit of a shock and encourage them to progress to pastures new avoiding doing too much damage. Knowing my luck though, they would more than likely go on and raid some other poor soul of their prize poultry. Looking back at this I ask myself the question, why did I not kill the lot? The answer to me is as clear now as it was then. I have always believed in having huge respect for our quarry species and hunting the fox is all about the word balance. That is why when the sport was at its very best we could proudly say, we had the most healthy fox population in Western Europe or more than likely the World. That is fact and something with which our opposition cannot argue.

The other days that week spent in Friday Woods meant coming in from different directions with little overlap as to where we had been on previous mornings. It became hard work as scent unfortunately did not match up to that of our first day, but success was measured on the way the hounds had performed and there was no doubt they were improving all the time. As we progressed through September and October the ground became incredibly hard and dry with hardly a drop of rain until ten days after the Opening Meet. Sore feet and lame horses had to be overcome, but as always when the rain arrived, it did not know how to stop. Late one very damp and dreary Saturday afternoon in November we decided to go and draw Bricett Park, a covert that the Essex and Suffolk Hounds had not drawn for many years. I had thought that it was owned by Mr and Mrs Cooper although it happened to be owned by the RAF. The Coopers had always been wonderful supporters and gave a very hospitable lawn meet. This was a day when George was hunting hounds, with Mary field mastering, it meant I could slip on and hopefully get a view which would prove helpful. As a result I was in the thick of the action as they soon found and within a few minutes a rather large fox appeared on the plough in front of me. He wasted no time whatsoever and was off, heading for none other than the married quarters of Royal Air Force Wattisham, a highly active base of the Phantom Bomber. The hounds were out of the covert in an instant and there was I can tell you no stopping them, not a chance. As they came away he was only fifty yards in front of them and seemed totally unfazed by the whole performance. After crossing a very large field our fox then disappeared into the garden of a rather smart looking house, followed in hot pursuit by the Essex and Suffolk Hounds.

The going was bottomless and the horse power that had begun to run out before we even went to draw was now done for altogether, so what next? Swift action was required, as all one could hear by now was them disappearing further and further into the depths of the base. George made his way up to the boundary fence in the hope that if he stood there and blew for long enough they would swing back to him. Well, eventually they did but it all seemed to take rather a long time. Meanwhile I said I would go and try and find the right person to speak to, so on dumping my horse with some kind soul, I managed to hitch a lift round to the main gate. The Airmen on duty must have received rather a shock when a dirty red coated individual turned up asking if he could have his hounds back. Luckily good humour prevailed, and after a few phone calls and radio messages from their colleagues, we found out that most of the hounds had gone back but four couple of them were in the dog pound. I rushed off to retrieve them and remember the airman in charge remarking that they were not very good on a lead. I then had the pleasure of being given permission to go and explain our misdoings to the person into whose garden they had disappeared and who happened to be none other than the Station Commander. Nervously knocking on his front door I had not the slightest clue what would happen next, would it be my turn to be impounded? After brief introductions, I was unexpectedly invited in. Thankfully I just about managed to heave my boots off without incident and was offered a seat which to my horror gave me a view through the window of his garden fence, or what little of it was left. Miraculously a glass of whisky appeared and then it was my turn to give evidence as to what had occurred just that hour before. Anyway after a long and very fruitful chat, the Station Commander admitted he had not heard much of what had been going on around him as there had been a rather good 'Dining In' night at the Officers Mess the night before and he had been sleeping off a hangover. All was forgiven, and with the CO offering to repair the fence, we could have come out of it a lot worse. In fact, little did we realise at the time but a long and very beneficial relationship between the RAF and Essex and Suffolk Hunt was just beginning and subsequent Station Commanders became very good friends.

The rest of the season progressed along nicely with the weather towards the latter part of January turning unseasonably mild. The hounds were continuing to improve and foxes were turning up in quite reasonable numbers and we achieved some very worthwhile hound hunts in both Essex and Suffolk. This was due to the farmers in both counties being very supportive and although shooting was an important part of their lives, they had never forgotten previous Masters, such as John Jiggens and Rowley Hitchcock. Both of them were great agriculturalists and immensely popular. Sadly John had died before I arrived in this part of the world but I was most fortunate Rowley became a great friend. He was an immense source of good advice, always offered with a wonderful sense of humour. I can see him now sitting in his armchair telling me of the fun they had over the years. How lucky was I to have his support in trying to replicate the good old days. There was none of the doom and gloom that occasionally goes with some ex Masters, which my father would aptly call vermin.

In the early part of February winter well and truly struck. The wind turned round to the East and we were soon to be in the grips of night time temperatures dropping down to minus seventeen. The roads were blocked and for a good week or so we were unable to leave the Kennels. When conditions marginally improved we decided to have a day or two just handy to home and on one of these we were honoured to be joined by Barry Todhunter, the famous Huntsman of the Blencathra. Barry was recuperating from an extremely serious accident, caused by a rock which came down on top of him as his hounds were marking high up on a fellside. Over thirty years later he is still hunting the Blencathra Hounds. What a tremendous demonstration of human resilience, and the fitness of the man became obvious to us all on this day with temperatures still well below freezing. It was important for hounds to go out as they were beginning to get restless so I decided that it made sense to take all forty couple of them to Constitution Hill and give them a chance to let off steam. This was a covert at the back of Hadleigh town which was an impenetrable mass of briars and gorse. It was a good find but not the easiest from which to get the hounds away from. I sent Barry out onto the top side with Ivor Bunch, who at the time was First Whipper In and Kennel Huntsman to Mr Vestey at the Thurlow, and as soon as I put hounds in, the pair of them took great pleasure in holloaing a rather stout customer away. Quick as a flash hounds flew to them and within seconds they had hit it off and were gone. I had much ground to make up and on getting myself at the top of the hill saw Mr Bunch and the badly injured Mr Todhunter striding out three hundred yards in front of me, effortlessly through the snow. Rock or no rock Barry and his companion kept going and with hounds now in top gear there was no hope of me catching them. I just kept plodding on until we reached some old gravel pits which again were a mass of brambles, where I finally caught up. The hounds were hunting well in the thick stuff and certainly didn't need me interfering in any way. After a while the fox slipped across into the Vice Chairman's garden and took refuge in a rather good breeding earth. This had been an exciting couple of hours. It was a day which we had been lucky enough to snatch from the elements and is one the three of us still talk about today.

As the season drew to a close we said farewell to my Joint Masters George and Mary. They both did a tremendous amount to get me going and I shall always be most grateful to them. Sadly Mary died in 1989, just two seasons after I left to go to the Fitzwilliam and is greatly missed by many foxhunters up and down the land. There were many reasons for this, but in particular Mary, a cross between a Tory and a Mitchell, both of whom were staunch hunting families, possessed instincts on a hunting day that were undoubtedly half fox and half hound, a huge help to her. I am quite sure, given the opportunity, she would have made a top class Huntsman.

Life was fine and I had much to look forward to in the coming seasons, with new Joint Masters and more fun to be had.

UNSUNG HEROES

There is a very large number of people who have over many years contributed greatly to the everyday running of our life in the countryside. They come from every corner of society and are to be admired each in their own individual way for the huge efforts they have gone to, to ensure that our living landscape and our traditions are safeguarded for future generations. They are our unsung heroes. If we were not to give them the coverage they deserve little would be known about them and their achievements. Some are enthusiastic supporters of the Chase and partake in the sport regularly. It is not necessarily the chosen activity of others, but somehow it has found a way to integrate itself into their life, in one form or another.

It is because these wonderful people are not household names that their life stories are so much more interesting to us. Bob Gosling, now 94, was born and brought up in a farming family in Suffolk. If there is anybody who could be a more perfect example of demonstrating the links that have existed over many years between agriculture and the hunting world, I have yet to find one.

Robert Gosling

12th November 1919

Only two words really sum up Robert (Bob) Gosling and in their own way they are totally sufficient. He is the most wonderful example of a 'True countryman' you could find. There is nothing that could describe him any better. Being one of those from the old school and now half way through his nineties, he alone will have seen more changes in farming and the rural way of life than many who are alive today.

His arrival into the world came just a week after the family arrived at Box Tree Farm, Hitcham, midway between Stowmarket and Hadleigh in the middle of what was then and still is today very much part of rural Suffolk. Born in the evening of 12th November 1919 and weighing in as he says at a strong 10lb, he had no hesitation in telling me this gave him a thoroughly good start in life. His father was Alfred and mother Rose, a member of the Underwood family who also lived locally.

The Gosling family farmed 84 acres of their own land with another 34 acres belonging to the Glebe close by. Agriculture at the time of Bob's birth was in the deepest depression and whilst the Goslings were indeed fortunate that they owned the majority of what they farmed, life for many was extremely tough. What made things worse was there was very little respite until the early '50s. The problem, as Bob explained, was that the Americans and the Canadians were flooding the UK with wheat and maize and it was far cheaper to import than produce it ourselves, therefore leaving British farming firmly in the doldrums. Thousands and thousands of acres were being left virtually unfarmed.

However having been brought into the agricultural world, that was where Bob was to spend the rest of his working life,

Bob Gosling (right) with colleague Jack Garrod receiving their Long Service Awards at the Hadleigh Show

and he loved it with very few regrets. He started school at five years old and in 1933 aged fourteen had left to go and help out his father. It is from here on that he vividly remembers not only those early days but the rest of his working life.

His first memories were of going off regularly to Bury St Edmunds Market with his father to buy calves. This they used to do by setting out in an Austin Cowley. Once the animal had been bought for anywhere between 10 to 18 shillings it was put in a pulp bag with the string carefully tied round its neck. It was then placed on the back seat of the car. On arriving home the calf would receive the Gosling treatment for settling the stomach which was a raw egg, shell and all straight down the throat. Whether it was cures for humans or their livestock, many of them have long been forgotten nowadays. However Bob does recollect the best cure for a chest infection and that was first to take three tablespoons of flour and one of mustard and mix them into a paste, then put the mixture into a pillow case, fold like a pancake and move round the chest and back for two days. He tells me that you were very soon better!

At that time most households were large and for many it really was a matter of living hand to mouth. There were bankruptcies everywhere. To ensure there was a plentiful supply of meat a lot of families kept a pig or two round the back of the house. This, with the huge number of rabbits that were about at that time, certainly helped to keep those living in Rural Britain free from hunger. Whilst his father kept a dozen or so sows, it was Bob's responsibility to grind the meal and ensure all their livestock were managed correctly. Livestock was worth hardly anything and if it had not been a family owned farm the end would have certainly come for the Goslings, like sadly it had for so many others not only in Suffolk but throughout the country. To make matters worse War was declared again on the 3rd of September 1939. Bob kept working on the land, whilst at the same time joining the Kettlebaston Home Guard which played an important part in defending the local area and especially RAF Wattisham from German attack.

In 1940, aged twenty one, Bob married Mabel who was the youngest of eleven children. They moved to Loose Hall at Hitcham where he had started work for the Morley family who also owned Clay Hill, Box Tree and Studdles Farms. As the need for food production increased he started contract ploughing with an Allis Chalmers crawler which had no cab. The exhaust was situated right in front of him with no such thing as a silencer, so you can imagine his ears must have been more than ringing after a long day's work. It astounds me after what he told me that he is not stone deaf.

In June 1943 a Mr Bert Steward came down from London's East End to Suffolk and bought Water Mill Farm in Nedging. He had run a fruit business but due to the Blitz quite understandably made good his escape. However he found rural life far from easy and within a year or two made his way back to where he came from. Early in 1947 a Major Taylor made his way down from Kirkudbright in Scotland in an Austin Seven to look at a farm near Newton Abbott in Devon. It was on his rather indirect way home that he decided to view the Mill and its surrounding land which in all added up to just short of a hundred acres. It seemed to suit the Major's plans. He bought the place and moved down in the late spring of 1947 employing the existing farm staff of Jack Garrod and Ted Day and a short while later Bob arrived on the scene.

Agriculture at that time was under huge pressure to produce enough to feed the Nation. Food was scarce and rationing was still very much in evidence. As a result of this a set acreage of potatoes and sugar beet had to be grown on each farm. To assist in this as well as the ploughing and drilling of arable crops the Major bought three Suffolk Punches, Prince, Sunlight and Brag. Whilst there were two small tractors, heavy horses were still a huge asset to the farming industry. All three men employed had their own responsibilities and one of Bob's was the hand milking twice a day of the six cows whose milk was sent off to Stowmarket Creamery. A new parlour was added and the herd was increased to a dozen.

Traditionally the whole local community would pull together at harvest. The wheat would be cut by binder and stooked up for ripening. When the thrashing machine arrived it was like a great gathering of the locals and everybody helped until the job was finished and done. It was then that much beer was consumed in celebration, with the good old fashioned harvest suppers taking place when all had been safely gathered in. They then returned to ploughing and sowing the following year's crop and milling enough stock feed for the winter months ahead.

Shortly after that first harvest at Nedging, Bob's father offered £300 for a 250 acre mixed farm which he thought would suit the family, only to have it turned down. Two months later it was sold for £275. This was something that would have been Bob's chance to farm on his own and is something that he still regrets to this day. However he never let this get the better of him and his loyalty to the Taylor family is as strong today as it ever was.

Although farming was going through a very tough time, hunting was and still is a very popular activity in this part of the world. This is Essex and Suffolk country where Ken Mason, whose family owned the local cement works at Great Blakenham, was Master. Major Taylor came from a hunting family whose connections were with the Badsworth in South Yorkshire and he not only welcomed the hounds but hunted regularly himself with the Essex and Suffolk, the Easton Harriers and other Essex packs.

As you can imagine not only would work come to a halt if the hounds were in the area as all the necessary earth stopping would have to be undertaken beforehand. Between them Bob and Jack decided that this was going to be their responsibility and they were paid five shillings each with a bonus of a pound if there was more than one fox on the place. This worked out well and they took on the stopping not only in Semer Wood but right the way across the neighbouring farms. Foxes were reasonably abundant at the time so this certainly would have helped both family's cash flow. What is more, as food was short, Bob in particular would use this opportunity to behave in a way that was not dissimilar to our vulpine friends. In fact he always said he liked to play the fox by returning home from stopping with the odd cock pheasant that had miraculously fallen from high up in a tree on a moonlit night. On occasions there may have been a hare or a rabbit hidden under his coat. The truth being that also hidden in the inside pocket was a 0.22 rifle which he had bought in Ipswich for £9!

At the end of each season the Masters would lay on a right feast for all their Earth Stoppers in the Hadleigh Town Hall. With great slabs of beef provided and a plentiful supply of beer an enjoyable evening was guaranteed.

This was a different era when rural communities knitted together much more than they do now and it is a time which Bob looks back on and describes fondly as the "Good old days." As the years progressed so has farming, both at Nedging's Water Mill, and everywhere else in the country. The dairy cows went and single sucklers were bought in. After a while this no longer became viable and the grazing on the low meadows was rented out. The arable land was and still is taken care of by a good neighbour, John Chaplin.

A year or two before Major Taylor's death both Bob and Jack became semi-retired and were presented with their long service awards at the Hadleigh Show by Sir Joshua Rowley. These were two men who committed themselves to agriculture for all but fifty years a piece. The changes they will have seen in what in the greater scheme of things is a very short time are quite remarkable. From three men working a hundred acre farm, with three heavy horses and two small tractors, to one man per thousand acres and the huge machinery that goes with it today, makes one realise just how advanced farming has become. However it is the knowledge and expertise of Bob's generation that has stood the test of time. When the Nation needed feeding they were the ones that took up the mantle and committed themselves to ensuring farming tackled the challenges that lay ahead. It is easy to forget but they are the ones who have quite literally helped agriculture develop into the position it is today.

Bob admits he is very lucky to be able to look back over the years with very few regrets. His knowledge of the countryside, nature and everything that goes with it has not only enhanced his own life but many others around him.

The Rev William Burke
Born 4th August 1946

When choosing William Burke for 'Unsung Heroes' I knew in my own mind he would be one of the most inspiring people I could ever have the privilege of interviewing. It is therefore my hope and belief that as you read his life story and hear about his work, you too will be greatly touched by his commitment, not only to the Churches that are his responsibility, but to the wellbeing of his Parishioners. I have every confidence that you will find him the same as I have - a truly remarkable person.

William was born in Redruth, Cornwall on 4th August 1946 to Alexander who was serving as air crew with the RAF in Burma, and Rachel who was Scottish and had lived in Perthshire before moving to Argyll and thence to Cornwall. William's early wish was either to become a Priest or a Shepherd out on the Trossachs. Although he has achieved this former desire, the nearest he has got to the latter is always ensuring there is a traditional breed of sheep grazing in the Churchyard. These are normally Black Hebredian or Soay, rare breeds contemporary to St. Kyneburgha, the Royal Abbess who was buried at the village Church of Castor, in the seventh century and is where William has now been the Rector for nearly 20 years.

Whilst his father was serving in Northern Ireland, William's school days were spent at Kings, Worcester where he tells me he did not excel. Some may think otherwise. However, as a nineteen year old he decided that a career in the army would be the ideal move, so in 1965 it was off to Sandhurst where in 1967 he was commissioned into the Inniskillings. During his time at Sandhurst he realised it had certainly been the right decision to join up and his life as a successful and most respected soldier was just beginning. William partook in the pleasures that both horse and hound can bring and hunting with the Staff College Drag, Garth and South Berks, Mr. Goschens, South and West Wilts as well as the Royal Artillery became an all important part of this

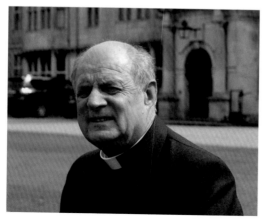

young soldier's recreational activities. The horses he hunted had plenty of experience and were supplied by the Mounted Infantry or the Garrison Saddle Clubs. On Wednesday afternoons whilst at Sandhurst Hal Chavasse, his Company Commander, ensured there was time for his men to enjoy some beagling. This was with the Army pack, the Sandhurst, whose hounds were kennelled in the grounds of the College.

Throughout the period 1967 to 1990 William served with various special service organisations but mainly with *The Rev William Burke enjoying the Fitzwilliam Puppy Show* the Inniskillings, which later became the Royal Irish Regiment. There were tours out to Northern Ireland, Germany, Cyprus, Belize and the South Atlantic and life was never dull for William. Suddenly, out of the blue, news came of the harrowing death of a colleague and very close friend. The circumstances of the death were to change William's life forever. The possibility of his early wish to join the Priesthood returned to him and was to become a reality. In his own words: "This was going to be something far flung from what it is like to be a regular soldier." At that time though, William knew in his own mind he was being called to the Church and deeply wished he had been at his friend's side at the time of his death.

Like many good soldiers, William's life until then had been entirely devoted to Queen and country. His life since, has been devoted to God and the Church as well as Queen, country and everybody around him. Being a thoroughly good man it made perfect sense for him to go off and study Theology which he did at Ripon College, Cuddesdon in Oxford. He was ordained in 1992 and it wasn't long before he, his wife Diana and their family found themselves in an Inner City Parish in Watford, where the biggest single ethnic group were Asian/ Muslims. It was an Anglo/Catholic Parish and was where William worked out the theology of his priesthood. This means dealing with people as you find them, accepting them as they are and seeing how one could help. His lasting memory of this period in Watford was being privileged to spend his time amongst what he describes as a really good solid group of hard working Parishioners, who were totally committed to the Anglo/Catholic tradition of the Church. In his typical warm hearted way William also worked closely with those from the Muslim faith, which he found to be most beneficial to both communities. He was Priest here for four years and sums this up by saying in this most humble way: "I really did learn more from them than they did me, you know."

In 1994 William met Sir Stephen Hastings and a while later was asked to lunch with him at Milton Hall, close to the City of Peterborough. Sir Stephen, as well as being a former MP and Master of Foxhounds, was the Patron of the Livings of Castor, Marholm, Sutton and Upton, which were in need of a Rector. After a while they agreed between them and a move was made from Watford to the Eastern Counties. The people and the whole area were totally new to William, but there have been, as you would expect, no regrets whatsoever. To leave the army was one thing, to go to an Inner City Parish was another, but to then up sticks again for parishes which were surrounded by one of the largest family estates in rural England was a different challenge again. The decision was made much easier for William, as one very special person committed herself to making his time here work. This was the Hon. Lady Hastings, fondly known as Lizzie Anne, a staunch Roman Catholic who was loved and adored by all who knew her, from whatsoever background they came. Looking back on those early years when the Burke family first moved, he remembers that Lizzie Anne became the most wonderful source of advice and support he could ever have wished for. Sadly only three years after they arrived, Lizzie Anne was diagnosed with cancer and whilst she fought it with great determination, it beat her in March 1997. A remarkable person and a truly great friend had been lost to all of us who lived and worked at Milton. As a tribute to her William arranged for all his Parish Churches to hold Roman Catholic Services, something of which she would have been hugely proud.

Whilst it became well known after Lizzie Anne's death that the foxes on her Milton and Wentworth Estates started to behave in a rather strange manner, William related to me the true but lesser known story of a hare. Lizzie Anne was a most enthusiastic Egyptologist and adored hares, so much so she always made sure there were cushions depicting this animal scattered all around the house. In the twelve years I was at Milton I never once saw one in the Park and I do not believe anybody else did. The Beagles and Bassets both hunted regularly up to the wall but no hare was ever seen crossing into the Park. It was not because they couldn't, it was just somewhere they didn't seem to go. However, two days after her death Sir Stephen was working at his desk when he happened to look up and there was a hare lolloping about on the drive in front of the house. Instead of running off, she came right up to the window. This, incidentally, was exactly the same place a fox was seen a day or two later. She then turned away and totally disappeared, seemingly into thin air. When Sir Stephen mentioned this to William he said with confidence that Lizzie Anne had sent a sign to say: "Don't be anxious, don't be afraid, I promise you I am alright." For two foxes and a hare to do the same thing is extraordinary and there is no doubting it makes us stand back and think. After this experience both Sir Stephen and William agreed that a hare should feature on her tombstone.

Life is never quiet with six parishes to look after and William's year is dominated by the seasons as he sees them: Christmas, Mothering Sunday, Easter, Harvest and Remembrance. The way that Christmas Eve is celebrated in Castor and Ailsworth is certainly a little different to most, and this is entirely down to William. For many years now the Fitzwilliam Hounds have met on the Green and as the hounds trot down to the Meet, William ensures the Church Bells are rung loud and clear to welcome them. This is the beginning of the celebrations and brings together a large crowd which fills the village green to overflowing with those wishing to savour this very traditional experience. Later that afternoon many of those who were at the Meet are there attending the family Carol Service. Under his watch this has become a most special occasion, with donkeys, sheep and even the odd camel taking part. He recalls the time when a lady, who had not been to Church for thirty five years, decided to go and take her grandchildren and the donkey stopped abruptly right in front of her, there was no budging it. Eventually it put its head forward and stared straight at her for a few minutes before deciding in its own time to move on. The certain lady is now a regular churchgoer.

The traditions of Castor and the surrounding villages are beautifully demonstrated on a tapestry which was created for the Queen's Jubilee. Village life, farming, and scenes of the Fitzwilliam Hounds in full cry have all been created into an eight foot by four foot piece of work, which hangs in the Church and is much admired by those who visit. The local fox has also found himself featured on it and so he should as he is just as an important part of life in and around there as everything else.

Each season has its own distinctive character and William makes the most of them by using different themes that will appeal to his congregation, which of course covers all different ages. He loves his work and as a result attendance at the Parish Churches of Castor, Marholm, Upton, Sutton and Water Newton, and Stibbington are very healthy. The input that goes on behind the scenes in organisation is what makes the difference between success and failure and the Church is no different. Whilst preparing for services takes up a considerable amount of time, Baptisms, Weddings, and Funerals all have to be fitted into the calendar, some of course at very short notice. William and his small team around him have to be well organised. There is one other ingredient of life in his Cambridgeshire Parishes which is hugely important and should never be overlooked, that of visiting the elderly and the sick, many of whom he will have known for a considerable number of years, through their working lives to retirement and old age. A call to see them, a cup of tea, and maybe a quiet moment of prayer makes all the difference to somebody living in lonely circumstances and William knows how much a visit means to them. I was reminded just how well respected he is by old and young alike when I called to see him recently. As we made our way to the pub we met some young people walking down the road. He knew them all by name and they knew him with smiles and a nod being exchanged. This not only tells us of the popularity of the man but just how important his role is in the life of the villages around him.

As William enters his final year in the priesthood, he looks back at his days which have been happily spent in the beautiful buildings and stunning churches of his parishes, in the company of generous people that work so hard for their community. To each and every one of them he is eternally grateful.

Horace Batten

Born 17th June 1912

To visit the works and shop of Horace Batten the Bootmaker Ltd is a remarkable experience. To meet the man himself and hear his life story and that of the business is even more so. Horace Batten was a hundred and two in June 2014 and is someone who has the incredible ability to remember in detail so much of what has happened over the years. He certainly makes a mockery of us who are half his age.

Horace Batten, the fifth generation of Bootmakers, was born on 17th June 1912 at Long Buckby in Northamptonshire, just a stone's throw from Ravensthorpe, where he and the business have been based for many years. From his early days he remembers the ethic of hard work being drummed into him. As well as the family owning and running the boot making business in Northampton, they also raised a large number of ducks and geese on their farm at Long Buckby, so there was never a day when there was nothing to do. Mr Batten certainly found this out, for being the only child there were no siblings with whom to share the daily responsibilities.

It is interesting to note the Batten family originate from Ilminster in Somerset where they were making boots and shoes at the time of the Civil War. In 1800 a Mr William Batten moved to Gloucester and then onto Hackney in London's East End where he continued to develop the business. However, while in Gloucester one of the family slightly deviated and became Chief Constable of the County. Then in 1910 they made their way to Northamptonshire and have been there ever since.

Three generations of the Batten Family

Horace's early memories are of an era long gone but never to be forgotten. Near their works in St Michael's Road Northampton there was a very large ammunition factory. Mr Batten remembers vividly towards the end of the First War lorries being loaded with six inch shells which were being taken away to be filled with gunpowder. Life in Northampton at the time was extremely hard, as it was everywhere, and it did not get any easier for a considerable number of years. The Batten family had decided that they were not going to go under, so some serious innovation was required. Horace's father, although being a very hard worker, was not a good businessman, so in 1931, whilst the country was still continuing to suffer the worst effects of the depression, the young nineteen year old Horace joined the company. The demand for hunting boots was still there but something desperately needed doing to galvanise the business into action. The decision was made to get out there and promote the fact that a lot of hunting boots which were made at this time didn't last, but that the Batten boots did. So with a hundred pounds that he had been left, he bought an Austin Seven and set off around the Hunt Kennels of England. Horace Batten always thought of himself as a bit of a rebel but he wasn't frightened of hard work. It was the approach of producing a high quality boot, and making people aware of the fact, which saved the day for future generations. I was fascinated to learn that his hunting boots were always made from a particular, special leather from Devon, and still are to this day. The leather is dressed on the flesh side and not the skin side, because the scratches can be boned out.

Mr Batten's memories of his kennel visits are as vivid as if they had happened yesterday. Huntsmen at the time he remembers were God and woe betide you if you happened to get on the wrong side of them. On one occasion he arrived at the South Notts Kennels to find that all the staff, Huntsman included, had walked out. However there were many happy memories of visits to Badminton, Brent Pelham, Barnby Moor and Chipping Norton where orders would have been taken and high quality boots made for the country's Masters and Hunt Staff. He has particularly fond memories of the Champion family, with Bob, Nimrod and Jack all coming from a long line of Hunt Servants.

Life away from visiting Hunt Kennels also had its amusements. Horace tells of one occasion when he was attending a service in what was the old Coventry Cathedral. The Bishop started ranting on about secularism. He got so fed up with it that he left his pew, took his bible and laid it on the floor in front of the pulpit, called him a clown and walked out. He decided afterwards that he ought to go back to his own Vicar and admit his transgressions who, he said: "Took it very well and just laughed it off."

In 1939 Mr Batten married Barbara who helped and supported him for many years in the business as well as being a wonderful housewife and mother to their son Tim who was born in 1945 and now runs the business with his daughter Emma. Barbara was very artistic and a real go getter. As well as helping to run Chelsea Flower Show, she started the National Association of Flower Arrangers. Mr Batten did not take part in active service when war was declared in September 1939, as he was the only man in the country who knew how to make Sea Boots. Production of these took priority over hunting boots and he was kept very busy throughout, especially as a whole year's supply had been bombed. It was also at this difficult time that Lady Reading, Head of the Land Army, needed stout footwear for the girls who were keeping farming going. Mr Batten had his own motto: "If he could, he would and sure enough he did." He made some solid hard wearing ladies boots, which replaced the "bloody silly shoes they were expected to wear." One of his sad memories of the war was when he turned up at the Cheshire Kennels just at the desperate time they were putting a lot of the hounds down. This certainly left its mark on him, as it did many others who were in Hunt Service at the time. It was wonderful though to think that hunting managed to continue in a limited form not only to keep on top of the fox population but to be there for those returning from the ravages of intensive fighting in Europe and the Far East.

After the War hunting became more popular with an ever increasing demand for proper quality hunting boots. Mr Batten's comments are interesting as they come from a man who has never hunted on a horse, but sees it as something more than a sport. To him it plays a very strong and active role in the countryside as well as keeping a healthy and well balanced fox population. These are wise words which certain politicians should listen to.

Horace tells me that boot making has kept the family together and that the business of boot making has rubbed off naturally on him. It is the hallmark of the Batten family. I am sure this is absolutely true, and coming from the fourth generation of a family which has hunted with hounds I can empathise with that remark.

Since 1931 he has travelled the length and breadth of the country. During those years he has met all types of Masters and Huntsmen, the vast majority of them he would describe as "Good chaps, but like in any business there are always one or two to whose standards are not what they ought to have been." Hunting, he believes, has tremendous support but he fears for the wellbeing of the fox, as everybody nowadays seems to have a gun. How right he is.

Whilst we were winding up this remarkable conversation I suggested it might be an idea if we could possibly take a few photos of the boss in his workshop. Quick as a flash he started to lift himself out of his armchair saying to Tim: "Come on then, anything for business"!

Close on one thousand six hundred words do not suffice when writing an article about such a character. It is only the very beginning. Thanks must go to you Mr. Batten for giving me the remarkable opportunity of at least going this far. It has been a real privilege and something I will never forget.

As an aside to this article Horace told me a little story about his father which you may find of interest. It was told to Mr Batten by his father. At 12 o'clock one autumn day in 1908 he sent a postcard from Long Buckby Station to his intended in London saying that he would pick her up at 7.30 that evening. The postcard was delivered to the London address at 4.30 that afternoon! How long would it take that very same letter now I wonder?

Richard Wright
Born 23rd May 1938

Richard Wright is the epitome of those who are the backbone of our countryside and what it stands for: hard work, dedication to high standards of agriculture, and being prepared to uphold our rural sporting traditions in a quiet and dignified way.

Richard Wright was born on 23rd May 1938, and is probably more modest about his achievements than most people I have ever met. His father and grandfather were both born and farmed at Oxey Farm, near Tilton on the Hill in Leicestershire, so it was more than likely Richard was going to venture into the family business. This he duly did and there are no doubts that over the years he has developed the farm into something of which his forebears would have been justly proud.

First memories of a farming life are often fascinating to listen to and having been born just sixteen months before War was declared, Richard has many of those. Farming at that time was under huge pressure to feed the nation having been in the doldrums for so long and the Wrights were determined to do their bit. It was

Richard and Di Wright with their prize South Devon Herd

not long before they managed to requisition some of the first Italian and German prisoners of war. One of the Germans, Fritz Berg, stayed with them for more than forty years and his son now works for the Allerton Trust who own and run the nearby Loddington Estate.

Farm machinery at that time was somewhat basic compared to today. The tractors of the time were Fordson Standards and had wooden frames. Anything rubber went to the war effort. Harvesting was still being undertaken by a binder and a large number of people was needed to stook up the sheaves for the threshing machine which would be fired into action a week or two later. It was hands on to get everything completed before autumn came round and drilling started again. In this part of the world, like the rest of Britain, every farmer by law had to grow a certain acreage of potatoes. In the eastern counties there was a requirement for sugar beet also to be grown, but in Leicestershire it was mangles for cattle or sheep feed.

Richard's school days were spent at Oakham. In his spare time he took evening classes in agriculture and became an active member of Tilton Young Farmers which as well as providing a good social life helped teach those participating how to judge livestock. Annual competitions were held and Richard took an active part in them, thus further enhancing knowledge which as time progressed was going to be incredibly useful to him. Tilton Young Farmers was also rather good at promoting its sporting activities with cricket and hockey very much on the agenda. However, as Richard recalls, for many, including he and Di, it will probably be most remembered for being the best marriage bureau in the county.

Oxey Farm at this time was 500 acres and produced 100 acres of wheat and 100 acres which would have been split between winter and spring barley, or oats, all of which was milled on the place. There were 10 acres of potatoes, the rest being pasture which supported a milking herd of Ayrshires and Friesian Cross Lincoln Reds as well as some beef cattle which had been reared on a bucket by Fritz Berg. They were taken right through to killing weight before ending up at Leicester Market. Some store cattle were bought which were finished at Oxey Farm and also sold at Leicester. The sheep enterprise consisted of anywhere between 300 to 400 ewes with lambs being sold as fat in Melton. In 1970, when bulk tanks came in, the cost of replacing the old milking system meant the cows had to go, and later the sheep followed. All this helped Richard considerably in concentrating on something that has become a key part of farming at Oxey since 1986 which was the formation of a beef herd of South Devons.

Starting with fifteen pure bred cows, Richard found the South Devon breeders extremely helpful and thus the herd started to grow rather more quickly than perhaps they first imagined. They were soon up to sixty and thought that was going to be enough, however some extra extensification payments in the late nineties helped increase the numbers further to two hundred spring calving cows, where it remains today. Richard's ambition is to end up with a polled herd without losing the size of their animals. There is no doubt he has gone a long way towards achieving this in what is, in cattle breeding terms, a relatively short time. They have become a vitally important part of what makes Oxey Farm tick and have undoubtedly been one of the main reasons why the Wright family are now responsible for farming two thousand acres of Leicestershire.

It is through their great interest in these wonderful traditional English cattle that both Richard and Di have made many good friends and with the South Devon Convention have travelled as far afield as Australia and New Zealand. On these visits they have been able to cast their expert eyes over a breed which is now equally well respected over there as it is here.

It looks extremely likely that farming at Oxey Farm is in the safest of hands with the next two generations of Wright's showing a real interest in Richard and Di's achievements. In Richard's typically modest way he says it is only because of having such a good team. All this is true, however without a good boss who has a deep and meaningful knowledge of what he wants to achieve then it can all so easily fall to pieces. There is no danger of that here. Son Geoffrey who at present is working in the financial sector is there in the background with the grandchildren, Arthur, Harriet, William and Philip already owning their own different forms of livestock. Richard and Di's daughters, Rachel and Susan, whilst not involved on a daily basis, are never far away.

Although Richard is not a hunting man, over the years he has done more than many in the support he has given the Cottesmore Hunt, serving on the Hunt Committee as well as having been Chairman and now President of the Hedgelaying competition. Their covert Loddington Reddish, from where many a good hunt has started, was also the place which supplied a constant source of ash rails. This has been invaluable in the repair work that is needed after the hounds have achieved a busy day in the hard riding Tuesday country. As well as all this Di found time to be District Commissioner of the Pony Club for ten years and they both helped to run the tote at the Point to Point.

Richard is first and foremost a shooting man and it is with his family and local farming friends that he has put together a proper sporting shoot. Numbers here are not the essential requirement, but quality birds. Enough are reared to be able to be out once a week throughout the season and with the terrain of the land lending itself to producing high and testing birds, good days are regular occurrences in this sporting part of the world. With Di picking up, and Richard and Geoffrey being out together, along with their friends, it is exactly what shooting is all about. It therefore gave tremendous pleasure to everybody out on a day last season to see father, son and grandson all shoot a pheasant on the same drive. Particular pleasure came from the fact that on this very occasion his grandson also shot his first pheasant. This was quite something for the family and will no doubt be remembered by them for many years to come.

Richard never went to agricultural college and he would openly admit that this is one of life's regrets. However this is a man who has not let it hold him back. With Di at his side their achievements at Oxey Farm have been outstanding by anybody's standards. Richard's instincts are that of a true agriculturalist as well as being the epitome of a proper sporting farmer. He is someone who manages to find the important balance that is needed in keeping the equilibrium exactly where it should be.

Agriculture, Field Sports, as well as your many friends and acquaintances from all over the world owe you, Richard, a great debt of gratitude for being a truly wonderful example of what being a good countryman is all about. It has been a privilege to write about you.

Doctor Alexander Walton MB BS MRGP

and

the late Mrs Christine Walton

This piece is breaking from the usual and covers the life stories of two remarkable people, both of whom are held in extremely high esteem, not only in their home town of Spalding, but throughout a large part of the Eastern Counties and beyond.

Alex Walton was born on 4th December 1941 at Kelloe in County Durham into what can only be described as a truly hardworking family. His father and grandfather were men of North Eastern mining stock and with it, proud of the fact that they were staunch Socialists and members of the Labour Party. Alex's mother came from a totally different background. She was from proper Lancashire farming stock and held traditional Conservative values. This would have made it a very interesting house in which to grow up. Alex's father was one of ten, with all his brothers going down the pit except for one who was sadly killed in the First War. He was spotted for having exceptional talent and was given the opportunity to study mining engineering at Sheffield University. On graduating he returned to Kelloe as Under Manager and was then promoted to Manager at Blyth Colliery in Northumberland and latterly to Wheatslade. It was always his ambition to become a Doctor but sadly this was not to be. He did however play a very important part in the North East Branch of the Miners Rescue, when an explosion ripped Wheatslade Colliery apart. It was a full eighteen months before they could reach where the bodies of their colleagues lay and when they did so the pit ponies bolted. This hit Alex's father very hard and was something he never got over.

Alex began his education at the Cathedral School in Newcastle before progressing to the Royal Grammar School, and then in 1960 to Medical School. Christine was born at Gosforth, near Newcastle on 18th October 1941 and lived there throughout her childhood. She was educated in and around Newcastle, firstly at La Sagesse Convent and then at Eastcliffe Grammar. Chris had also decided that the medical profession was where she wanted to be. She trained initially as a Cadet Nurse at the Royal Infirmary before qualifying as an SRN in 1963, a position which no longer exists. It was during their training at Newcastle General Hospital that Alex and Chris met. Trainee Doctor Alex and Trainee Nurse Chris were on the same ward when an enema needed to be performed. Possibly rank was pulled because Chris undertook the job, with the offer of being taken out for a glass of Babycham when they were next off duty. She duly accepted and in 1965 they were married.

On qualifying Alex continued to practice at Newcastle General before the two of them left to go to Edinburgh. While they were there Chris became a Night Sister and Alex was busy teaching medical students. They returned to Newcastle, with Chris going to the Royal Infirmary as a research Nurse to Professor Johnson and Alex back to the General where he worked on the baby wards. It was at this time that Chris was asked to read a medical paper to the Royal College of Surgeons, of which she will always be justly proud.

Dr Alex Walton and his late wife Chris at a meet of the Fitzwilliam Hounds

In 1970 it was time for change. Alex and Chris Walton decided that a new life beckoned and moved to the Market Town of Spalding in Lincolnshire. Having been brought up in the North East this was a far cry from what they were used to in and around Newcastle and Edinburgh. However as they were both fully qualified they were more than ready for the challenges that lay ahead of them. Alex joined general practice with a team of three other doctors. It was the duty of the Doctors from their partnership to attend casualty every other day as well as being responsible for playing their part in looking after the 30 bed maternity unit at Spalding Hospital. At this particular time their team of four looked after nine thousand patients in an area that spread at least eight miles into the Fens. Nowadays the number has risen to more like twenty thousand.

Alex vividly remembers his first night on call. Very late that night a distressed mother called about her new born baby who was showing signs of being far from well. For this young city doctor to set forth late at night into the wildness of the fens was something he will never forget and without any doubt left its mark on him for a number of reasons. After much searching he eventually found the house where mother and child were located and all turned out to be well. It was the journey back as dawn was breaking that the Fens started to spring into life with hares, rabbits and pheasants and even a heron all appearing on the road in front of him. This one experience well and truly demonstrated to Alex just how much their lives had changed.

On another late night call, to a man who had lost his finger in a pea viner, Alex was brought face to face with the importance of agriculture to the area, so being off duty the following morning he made a point of visiting the farmer where the incident had occurred. Alex wanted to know more about what the pea viner actually did. After some instruction and a trip round the farm he had a much clearer idea about farming here and as a result of this he developed two questions which he regularly used. They were: "How're things lifting and how're things selling?" The answer to both would always be the same: "Badly!" It was during this visit that the farmer asked Alex if he rode, as they were looking for someone to help exercise their horses. The reply was in the negative but Chris had done so in the past. Little did he know it at the time but he had been talking to Rex Sly, the Joint Master of the Fitzwilliam. From that moment on a firm friendship began and it is one that has been ongoing for over forty years. Chris became the stable jockey, and rode out regularly with Steph, Rex's wife. In due course she bought a horse, Rebel, and was introduced to hunting, something she greatly enjoyed and was to become an important part of her life for many years afterwards.

Whilst Alex continued to work hard in the Practice, Chris certainly did not sit still. Their daughter Sarah was born in 1972 and it was not only the duties of a mother and a housewife she performed. In her own right Chris like Alex was becoming immensely popular in the town with nothing being too much trouble for either of them. The role of JP, Chairman of the local Bench as well as Chairman of the North Sea Camp Board of Prison Visitors were just a few examples of her dedication to the local community. Alex in the meantime was fully engrossed in ensuring the best for his patients. He felt that it was important for young doctors coming to the area to have a better knowledge of the agricultural industry and the dangers that went with it. He therefore decided to create courses which would give their participants a far better understanding. This meant taking them out onto farms as well as to food processing and distribution plants. This was something that became a key part of their education and for many it was a totally new experience. Whilst on one of these visits he came across one of his patients who he had helped wean off the dreaded Valium. When he saw her cutting cabbages for coleslaw with the most lethal looking knife he felt perhaps it was understandable why he had put her on that form of medication in the first place. Most interestingly the lady concerned was married to a Ukranian prisoner of war who couldn't go back because the Ukranians had fought with the Germans against the Russians.

Doctors hours are long, tiring and can be extremely taxing, therefore some light entertainment is important to build into the schedule from time to time. Initially a day or two's shooting was on offer which Alex thoroughly enjoyed and whilst partaking in this met many of the local farming community. He then joined a syndicate and shot for fifteen years. This gave him the chance to enjoy the fens in the middle of winter, not always the most hospitable of places as those of us who know it quite well have found out. Fishing and skiing holidays also came into the equation and next it was Alex's turn to be introduced to hunting, perhaps something that all those years before when practicing as a medical student in the North East would never have even entered his mind. His first day was with the Fitzwilliam in the snow at Raunds near Wellingborough. A large glass of whisky helped calm the rather fragile nerves and then he was told by Rex Sly who was Master at the time to follow him. A large hedge suddenly loomed up out of the blue and the next thing he knew he was over it and away. This was such a memorable day for Alex, and the beginning of a new chapter in his life - hunting!

It was unfortunate for both Alex and Chris that because of their medical knowledge much of their time whilst out with the Fitzwilliam was spent picking up those who had just met the ground coming up to them rather quicker than they had wished for. It was however hunting that gave them the opportunity to enjoy something together. Many happy days were spent in the Fitzwilliam country as well as others and when the hounds went visiting Alex made sure to take time off. After all he was Senior Partner by now so why shouldn't the good doctor have some time to be allowed to enjoy the spirit of the chase? There was a day visit to the Grove and Rufford from where it is believed he got the bug, then the five day trip when hounds went to Salisbury Plain to hunt by kind invitation of the Royal Artillery. Lastly it was a week's Staghunting on Exmoor when the Master of the Fitzwilliam at the time felt a visit there was not the safest thing to do without a doctor being present. As he was the only one who had not hunted in the area at the time Alex accepted the invitation. The rest of that particular week turned out to be a most interesting addition to his hunting life.

Alex and Chris continued to hunt for several more years but have now retired both from practice and sadly hunting as well. They are a couple who from the very beginning have been there constantly devoting their lives to helping and supporting others. However it is they who have had more than enough thrown at them, either by accidents or ill health and yet through the incredibly caring nature they possess have always had other people's interests at heart. "How are you?" Alex or Chris would say, when you know only too well, it was they who were the ones you should be saying it to. The measure of the man is summed up, I believe, by this: having retired and not been in the best of health Alex took on the Chairmanship of the Spalding Branch of Help the Aged and actively looked at raising as much money as he could for them. That speaks volumes. Mention the name Walton in Spalding and I know for a fact you will not find anybody held in higher esteem than them.

It is not only the people of the town of Spalding that took to this couple from the urban North East to their hearts. It is time for us who are privileged to have been brought up in more rural surroundings to say, thank you Alex, thank you Chris, the kindness you have shown to all of us will never be forgotten.

James "Jim" Roy Meads

Born 9th July 1930

The legendary hunting photographer Jim Meads was born on 9th July 1930 at Barnet, in what was then semi-rural Hertfordshire and is now part of North London. His father Frank had flown Bristol Fighters at the end of the 1914/18 War and his mother Elsie was the daughter of the Chief Fire Officer in Barnet. Jim was one of three children with a brother, Roger and a sister named Heather as she was born whilst father Frank had been away photographing Grouse Shooting and had returned home with some heather attached to the grille of his car.

Pauline and Jim Meads

Whilst working in the family photography business, Meads and Payne, Frank took on the role of Staff Photographer for country Life. His time there was spent covering gardening in the summer months and hunting during the winter. In 1935 the family moved to Essendon in what was to become the country hunted by the Enfield Chace, following the disbandment of Major Smith Bosanquet's hounds. During the Second War Frank went from here to work as an Aircraft Inspector at De Havilland's in nearby Hatfield where they were building Mosquito Bombers. In 1944 their house and the village school was blown up by the German flying bomb - the Doodle Bug. This left no option but for the all the Meads family except Father to be evacuated to Aberdare in South Wales. Whilst they were there Jim went to Aberdare Grammar School to continue his education. After the War Frank left De Havilland and carried on as a freelance hunting photographer, which of course put the name of Meads very firmly on the map. In 1956 he published his first book *They Meet at Eleven* with Jim later going on to produce many others along a similar theme.

On returning to Essendon he joined the Enfield Chace Pony Club and was taught to ride by the legendary Miss Middleton who was renowned for her expertise in encouraging the young, including such well known names as Tom Hudson and Raymond Brooks Ward. Between them they begged and borrowed ponies so they could enjoy their hunting with Tim Muxworthy and Ted Cox who had come across from the Warwickshire. Although the country was very close to London they never thought of it as suburbia, which much of it is today. Memories of lawn meets given by famous names such as Barbara Cartland and Lord Salisbury at Hatfield House and others who lived in the area is something that Jim remembers well.

Leaving school in 1945 it was time to follow father to De Havilland where he went as a trainee photographer. A lot of flying air to air work was on the agenda, with Jim taking eight flights in a Halifax Bomber with such great pilots as the legendary Group Captain 'Cats Eyes' Cunningham. This was a memorable part of his early life which also had one major bonus in that he did not have to work on Saturdays, giving him the chance to become the 'Hunting Photographer on a Bicycle', again following in father's footsteps. In 1946 he attended his first Peterborough Royal Foxhound Show and has been fortunate to have missed only one since. That was in 1969 and was by default as he was asked to captain the Queen Mother's cricket team, as David Nicholson had broken his leg. In 1965 the last Hound Show was held at Eastfield Road, in Peterborough itself, and Jim was there to record the Heythrop winning the Champion of Champions Cup.

Jim recollects having to line up my great grandfather, grandfather and father on the steps of Brent Pelham Hall in 1947 to celebrate the season that all three were Masters of the Puckeridge together. It looks as though my poor great grandfather was already dead and had been stuffed especially for the occasion, however he was still very much alive and did go on for some while afterwards. I even have it on good authority that it was definitely Jim that took the photograph but Frank was the one that signed it. Jim also came to Brent Pelham in 1959 when I was born to take photographs of the new born child who he told me would not keep still. In the summer of 1989 his services were again required when our eldest son Ben was just six months old. It is believed his behaviour was somewhat better than that of his father. It has been a great privilege for us that he has photographed five generations of our family.

Jim joined the RAF in 1948 and hoped that he might become a pilot or possibly even venture back into air to air photography, but instead he ended up being a lorry driver for two years, after which he left the forces and went back to join his father in the family business. It was at this time that he continued to take the photographs with father Frank still signing them whilst taking the money as well.

Jim was most fortunate to marry the lovely nurse Pauline Franklin in 1956. She had been born in the East End of London within the sound of Bow Bells and as she says hunting was definitely not her cup of tea. However her opinions changed as they would have to if you were living with Jim and Pauline went on to learn to ride, again with Miss Middleton's help, before starting teaching and then the children coming along in 1958 and 1959. Jim describes Pauline as a more than tolerant wife of a hunting enthusiast. Having had the great fortune of meeting her I think that remark is more than true.

Jim carried on his hunting from a bicycle for a while before progressing to a motorbike which helped to get him known further afield. After attending his first Badminton, eventing and point to pointing were soon on the list of the subjects he covered. In 1958 he became hunting photographer to The Field working alongside Sir Andrew Horseburgh Porter, their well known and respected reporter. This helped him become more financially sound as at the same time he was still working for his father from Monday to Friday and Saturdays were put aside for his hunting work. Sundays were spent from seven in the morning to three in the afternoon processing and captioning pictures before despatching them on the old Red Star train from Hatfield to London to meet Monday's deadline. How times have changed.

On 13th September 1962 something was to happen that was to change the Meads' life forever. Pauline went off that morning with a friend for the day to London and left Jim in charge of the children. He decided it was a good idea to take them to watch the planes doing their routine exercises at Hatfield. He never normally took a camera on these occasions, however on this day he did. One minute the family were watching a Lightning jet flying perfectly normally, the next it dropped vertically out of the sky. Quick as a flash Jim grabbed his camera and took a photo of the whole event, which included a rather startled man on a Fordson Major tractor who was mowing grass. With the obvious shock as to what was happening around him he was standing up and looking the wrong way round. Little did Jim realise at the time that this was to become the Photograph Of The Year, not only here in the UK but throughout the World. The Pilot and Navigator were fortunate enough to eject safely and other than a written off aeroplane all was well and no lives were lost. However in another strange twist to the tale, Jim's neighbour, whose wife had gone to London with Pauline, had been due to fly that particular plane, but decided for some reason at the last minute not to do so. Pauline and her friend were most concerned as they had already seen newspaper hoardings at Kings Cross Station that there had been a bad plane crash at Hatfield. They were met by Jim running up the platform gesticulating with his thumbs up that everything was OK. Not only was there a satisfactory ending to this near tragedy but the whole event made Jim's financial situation much easier and allowed him from then on to go it alone, which was something that had always been his ambition.

In 1965 when the boys were still young the family moved to Westbury in the Grafton country, midway between Buckingham and Brackley. Jim took up the position of weekly columnist to Shooting Times and country Magazine, when hunting and shooting were looking at the effects the two sports were having on each other and how they could benefit from working more closely together. Experiments took place on both the Batsford Estate in Gloucestershire and the Thurlow Estate in Suffolk. Both these proved very successful and a lot was learnt from them. A trip to Tunisia to photograph wild boar shooting was another of his more exciting excursions to foreign climes.

In 1973 Michael Clayton, who was hunting with the Old Surrey and Burstow at the time, was asked to become Editor of Horse and Hound. Jim and Michael formed a great working relationship, hitting it off from the start. The two of them travelled all over the World visiting packs large and small with their weekly exploits being reported in Foxford's Hunting Diary, a column which was created by Michael when taking on his senior role. In 1974 Jim had saved enough money to buy a ticket for himself to travel to the States. The mutual respect they have for each other is remarkable. Over the years he has photographed many of the greats and their hounds, and for the initial introduction he will always be incredibly grateful. Without it life would have been somewhat different to say the least. To demonstrate this fact Jim tells me that, at the age of 83, he has visited the States 183 times. Wherever he goes, whether here or in the States, he is welcomed with open arms. If ever there had been an ambassador elected to the sport of hunting Jim Meads would certainly have received a very large percentage of the vote. Working hard up till 1985 he then decided that a move was to be made, not to where they had initially planned - Charleston in South Carolina - but Carno in Mid Wales in the heart of the David Davies country. They settled here and have become key members of their local community.

If taking it easy was what Jim intended to do then think again. Since 1990 he has never stopped travelling and he continues to write for our own as well as the American Sporting press which includes, In And Around Horse country with a regular article titled, *From across the Pond.* As well as this he has not been slow off the mark in producing a number of books which are packed full of his photographs from wherever he has been in the world. These include, They Still Meet at Eleven, They Will Always Meet at Eleven, My Hunting World, In Full Cry, Going Home, and Good Night Masters. In two of these books Jim was honoured to have the forewords written for him by His Royal Highness the Prince of Wales.

If that were not enough, when I tell you that in 2010 he went on to achieve something that no one has ever done before, and that was to have hunted with 500 different packs, it is then you know we are dealing with somebody completely out of the ordinary. The 500th pack was the Louden West in the USA and it is believed that great celebrations took place both before and after hunting.

At Peterborough Royal Foxhound Show in 1996, Jim was presented by Hunt Staff from all over the world with a wonderful Joy Hawken painting of himself crouching down and taking a photograph of some winning hounds. Then in 2009 he was presented by the Americans at Virginia Hound Show with a marvellous bronze for services to hunting worldwide.

He has many memories which stand out, however his greatest will be achieving hunting with 500 different packs of hounds. The most touching part about all this is that he knows that he could not have achieved any of it without the love and support he has received from Pauline, a remarkable lady in many very different ways. Pauline we salute you. You have both had to overcome quite substantial hurdles in your lives and the respect and admiration you are held in is plain for all to see.

So as we look back on Jim's career we can see in our mind's eye this tall gangly fellar finding his way across country like no other, knowing when to stop and put himself just in the right place to get the next shot. This is the hallmark of Jim. Here is a man who in the 21st Century has total disregard for digital photography and computers and still processes all his Fuji film himself. Jim tells me his secret is dedication, anticipation and concentration. There is no doubt that when James Roy Meads was born they threw away the mould.

Robin Leach

Born 16th January 1939

To visit Robin Leach and be able to talk about his life was not only remarkable but an absolute privilege. In September 2011 he was taken ill during the night, after having come back from setting up the sheep pens for Moreton Show. It was thanks to his dogged determination to survive, coupled with the care his family and the nurses gave him, that he is not only still here to tell the tale, but largely back to good health.

Robin was born at Great Barrington in Gloucestershire on 16th January 1939, not many months before War was declared. His father was a baker, and his grandfather farmed at Great Barrington and helped Robin on leaving school to develop a real interest in the dairy industry. Agriculture was very definitely in his blood. His Mother's family had decided to leave farming in Cumberland and relocate to Warwickshire in 1900. During the depression Lord Willoughby de Broke encouraged people to take farms on the Compton Verney Estate. As a result they put everything they owned, be it sheep, cattle, farm equipment or heavy horses on the train and arrived at Kineton Station on a late autumn evening just before midnight, quite an operation by modern day standards, never mind what it would have been like over a hundred years ago.

In 1960 Robin had the opportunity to buy Bobble Farm, Little Rissington and he was able to set up his own dairy herd of Friesians and Jerseys. He dedicated his life to hard work and milking twice daily. This quite rightly was not a job that he liked to leave to anybody else. However as time progressed hunting and particularly beagling managed to be fitted in around Robin's farming responsibilities.

Little Rissington is situated in the heart of the Heythrop country and in the 1960s Captain Ronnie Wallace was in his heyday. The hounds would more than likely have been out five days a week and the whole exercise was run like clockwork. Charlie Parker was Terrierman at the time and he took the young Robin under his wing. Charlie was a tremendous naturalist who knew much about wildlife in all its different forms, and Robin found him fascinating not only to talk to, but that learning from him was a privilege in itself.

As well as some of the best foxhunting in the country on the doorstep, the renowned Dummer Beagles, which had been established in 1939 by Sir Newton Rycroft in Hampshire, were also now kennelled in the village. Geoffrey Craghill, a lecturer at the nearby Royal Agricultural College, was Master with Dick Meyrick. The pair of them, along with their long serving Kennel Huntsman Charlie Smith, encouraged Robin to start whipping in. 1966 however will be remembered for two major events in Robin's life: it was the year he married Viv and it was the time that he started hunting the hounds. In 1977 he became Joint Master and for the next thirty seasons ran the Dummer to great success both in the field and in the showing ring.

Robin never rode but he took great pleasure in telling me that there is nothing quite like hunting a pack of beagles. It is all absorbing and gives you the chance for far better contact with the hounds. This is exactly what you need, he says, "to make a proper job of it." It is also his deep interest in the real art of venery that has never left him and as he explains: "The hare has the appearance of being like a soft animal with big ears, and although she is a herbivore looks, to say the least, can be deceiving." The advice he gives to any young huntsmen is always well worth listening to. For example, if your hounds have come to a check always make sure you cast an eye back over your shoulder, as very often your hunted hare will be sitting right behind you. As he explains hares will often double back on themselves, and sometimes for a considerable distance will run a tarmac road. This, along with their ability to go to ground, some may say, backs up the rumour that an "old hare is cleverer than a fox." One thing is for certain, whatever the truth happens to be they know every trick in the book.

For many livestock farmers who have hunted hounds the breed they are working with and its development is indeed a fascinating subject and as a result there are many contributing factors which are of paramount importance. For example nose, cry, stamina, agility and confirmation all need to be taken into consideration when breeding hounds, and the beagle is no different. The Dummer being an all bitch pack have long had an association with the Royal Agricultural College and the two have often used each other's blood. Hunting in these two parts of England is in many ways very similar, and so it is a great advantage to both packs. However it is interesting to note that when the Dummer have gone up to Northumberland in the past they seem to demonstrate just what a good pack of hounds they really are. The hill hares and their hounds have often in the past been known to disappear for miles into the distance on a good scenting day.

It is the memories of the really good days that fortunately never fail to leave us, and for Robin there was one particular day in February 2005 when the Dummer bitches pulled off a remarkable performance. With more than six miles of the North Cotswold and Heythrop country covered, the hunting on that occasion was exceptional. David and Dawn Minett kindly gave the meet at Downs Farm, Blockley. Before moving off a presentation was made to John Jones, the retiring head keeper at Batsford, who over the years had done so much to promote unity in field sports, especially between hunting and shooting.

Finding a hare fairly swiftly on the home farm, a good hunt around Blockley Banks took place before the hare crossed the Blockley to Bourton-on-the-Hill road and was caught after thirty minutes on the edge of Bourton Wood. They then drew the banks on Robin Dales farm and soon found lots of hares. After some inconclusive hunting they settled onto a strong customer who took them at a fair pace down to Ben Lovesey's farm, swinging back left handed nearly to Worcester Approach, then onto the Deer Park and the Sally Beds where she was nearly caught. However she made good her escape and went back over the Avenue, up Robin Dales banks and crossed the road to the left of Worcester Approach. They sped on over Holly Walk past Park Farm nearly to Cadley and over the Draycott road and on down to the brook which she crossed and on over the Blockley to Paxford road. Going on past Blockley village they caught the hare in a small spinney on the edge of Northwick Park. This had been a truly great hunt of 75 minutes. Only their road patrol was anywhere near them and Steve Duckmanton, their long serving huntsman, only just managed to keep in touch after requisitioning a quad bike. This day is testament to the hard work and dedication of Robin Leach and a great team at the Dummer.

Hunting, and in particular beagling, owe Robin a tremendous debt of gratitude for the wonderful contribution he has made over many years to the sport. The award he received from the Association of Masters of Harriers and Beagles demonstrates without doubt a sense of commitment which has been a very fine example to us all.

Thank you Robin. What a pleasure it has been to hear that a certain Robin Leach is still very much in evidence with the Dummer. Long may this continue to be the case.

Colonel Donald Easten MC

Born 15th July 1918

Colonel Donald Easten is one of the most distinguished characters from the Second World War left today and to be allowed to write about his life is a most remarkable privilege. I hope as you read this you, like me, will realise just how much we owe all those who fought so gallantly in both Wars, for the freedom we so enjoy today.

Born in Chislehurst, Kent at a time when the First World War was nearing its end, Donald's early memories of military life are as vivid in 2014 as they were almost ninety years ago. Those six horse teams of guns, hacking down from Woolwich to train on Chislehurst Common, unknowingly left an impenetrable mark on this potentially very brave young soldier. Donald liked to follow them on his bicycle and would then sit for hours and watch them practising with the heavy gunfire they would later require when they were called up for further action. Military training was very much part of everyday life in that part of England at the time and what he quietly observed stood him in good stead for the ensuing years in the forces.

It was whilst growing up here that the Royal Artillery Draghounds would also make an appearance in the village, being kennelled at the Barracks at Woolwich. The West Kent Foxhounds and the Bolebroke Beagles were close by too and this is where Donald's lifelong interest in hunting began. He had to pay to follow the beagles but as it was free to follow the foxhounds on foot, it was they who became his favoured choice of activity for a while. During his early school days at Bloxham, on the borders of the Heythrop and Warwickshire, many a happy hour was spent skiving off to hunt with either one or other pack. Lord Willoughby de Broke was Master of the Warwickshire at the time and it was he who not only encouraged many of the younger generation but was also responsible for the quote: "For hunting to survive it must be totally and utterly inclusive and if it wasn't it would lose its reason for being there." Wise words indeed and something Donald was certainly to practice during his long stint in the beagling world that was to come later in his life.

On finishing his education Donald went into the City and joined the Norwich Union as a junior clerk, staying with them until war broke out in September 1939. During this time he had joined the Territorial Army and served with the Honourable Artillery Company. The HAC was a unit committed to producing officers of the highest calibre, because during World War I they were sent into battle as an 'ordinary battalion', without a lot of training and a very large number of potential officers were lost. To Donald this showed that the army had listened to what had happened and learnt from those tragic circumstances. In 1940 he was commissioned as an officer and was posted to Northern France. These are his own words describing the situation: "At the time it appeared to us that we were going the wrong way as the others were all returning from Dunkirk!" So it was off to Dover for a while to be based at the Citadel and here he and his unit served under a rather flamboyant commanding officer who one day announced: "If there are any officers left when the Germans arrive, we will

die together under the flag!" When asked if any of them had any questions the Quarter Master quickly replied: "That's all very well Sir, but we haven't got a flag."

Donald was then posted to the Queens Own Royal West Kent Regiment and sent on a course to Sandhurst where he joined the 44th Division. Almost straight

Donald Easten (right) with his great friend David Hindle

away he was sent out to the Middle East and the Western Desert. However, on exercise just before they left, Donald happened to be lying in a muddy Kent field, when Montgomery and his ADC appeared out of the blue. The ADC came across to Donald and said that Montgomery had requested he become his second ADC. Donald soon responded, saying he could do no such thing until he had at least been shot at. The reply came back: "Quite right too!" Any lack of action whilst at Dover was soon reversed when Donald and his unit went into battle at Amal el Halfa. This was a relatively short campaign which preceded Alamein and was an attempt by the Germans to quickly try and outflank the Eighth Army. Happily this didn't work and so with no respite, it was straight into the Battle of Alamein with Montgomery very much in charge of operations. A little while later, when lying in a trench in the desert with a bad dose of dysentery, Montgomery's ADC suddenly appeared again. Donald was in a bad way and Monty's ADC was instructed to take him back initially to Eighth Army Headquarters and then on to the shores of the Mediterranean where he was to stay in one of the famous caravans to give him time to recover. After a week there were still serious concerns for Donald's health and Monty came around to see him and decided he should be sent to see the Full Colonel Doctor in Alexandria. He returned from there with a note, only to be sent back to hospital for further recuperation. By this time Donald had undertaken the journey three times at seventy miles each way. He was finally discharged and sent back to the Headquarters of the Eighth Army to ensure his health continued to improve, which it did, and it was not long before he was back in the action.

With the all important role of Liaison Officer he was soon sent out to Iraq, then to Egypt before returning to Baghdad. Donald's Commanding Officer at the time was someone with a very deep faith and as a result he ensured that they stopped at all the sites of religious significance. The arrangements for the visits were made by the sergeant who, on arrival at a certain spot, would instruct the lads in his own amusing way by announcing: "Come on now out you get lads, more of that Jesus stuff." They were in Iraq for three months where nothing happened, and then transferred to North East India. It was here that life changed dramatically and on reaching Kohima they were to find themselves under siege for two weeks, totally surrounded by the Japanese. The Japanese were then trying to force a way through from Burma into India. With concerted effort and great determination the British Second Division eventually managed to fight their way through and eventually lift the siege, although at great expense to human life. This had been one of the bloodiest battles of the Second World War and the number of British casualties was extremely large to say the least. It is said that an army should never march on an empty stomach, let alone fight, so when Donald and his men found some cattle grazing between enemy lines, this was fair game and it was not long before one was in their cook house.

The time was approaching when the beginning of the end of the War was drawing near, however they continued to push the Japanese right back to Rangoon and the danger to India ceased. In Rangoon, after continuous action, the news came through that it was all over. It was not too long before celebrations commenced with forty gallon drums of rum being brought in and consumed. Donald admits that he was to enjoy his fair share and this was just as well, as during the party, he happened to find himself being sawn in two by an Indian Concert Party who had been in the area and decided to join in. Afterwards he felt so drunk that for a while he could not remember a thing about what had happened, let alone how they had won the battle, or even the war for that matter. His actions during those last few months had not gone unnoticed though and as a result he was awarded the MC for two separate acts of bravery, one at Arakan and the other at Kohima. This tells us a great deal about Donald Easten and the men he led into battle.

Once the celebrations were over, they transferred by assault craft to Singapore, only to find the Japanese already there. They were bowing and scraping and obviously deeply upset, saying: "Oh dear, we are so sorry, we fought on the wrong side." He will never forget this occasion for it was when his opposite number in the Japanese Army approached Donald, drew out his sword and proceeded to present him with it. It is something he is proud to still have in his possession. After some mopping up duties Donald returned to England but continued his soldiering with the Queens Own Royal West Kent's until 1948. He was then transferred to the Royal Army Service Corps and for a while was based at Taunton. The Bolebroke Beagles, although kennelled in Kent, became very much part of his life again, and whilst on leave from Taunton he enjoyed many happy days with them. This of course was the pack that he had first hunted with as a child, all those years before. After eight years as a Full Colonel, Donald was then transferred from Taunton to Kempston in Bedfordshire which allowed him more time to devote to beagling, and it wasn't long before he became Master of the North Bucks. This was a position which he much enjoyed, especially when hunting the hounds which he undertook with great success for three seasons. In 1973 he retired from full-time soldiering and was appointed to a retired officer's job on the staff of the Eastern Region of the Army and Combined Cadet Force, which at the time was based at Colchester.

The Army had their own pack of Beagles here, namely the Colchester Garrison which later amalgamated with the Sproughton Foot to become the Stour Valley. It seemed most appropriate that Donald should be appointed initially as sole Master and then Joint. Donald hunted hounds on Wednesdays and Peter Ellrich, who had come from Badminton, on Saturdays and here he experienced his greatest memories of beagling. He describes the beagles as being like a lot of schoolboys being let out of school for the day and his green coat acted as a magnet to his hounds, in the same way a pretty young lady in a short skirt does to a group of young fellars! For fifteen years Donald committed himself to very high standards as one would expect from such a man. His advice for anyone wanting to become a Master in the twenty first century is as important today as it was then. "The farmers, landowners, and those that live and work in the countryside, whatever their occupation, are the ones who must be looked after in the proper manner, and this must be remembered at all times, for they are the core of the hunt and hunting overall. We ignore them at our peril."

Whilst hunting at Tolleshunt Darcy in Essex one day, the hounds had run onto land where they were not meant to be. The concerned farmer arrived in a bit of a hurry and came face to face with Donald who started to apologise but was soon told: "I am not worried about you beaglers it's those b..... foxhunters that bother me."

Donald is and has been a man of intense bravery who dedicated himself to his country in a way that all of us today should be deeply grateful. If ever there was any one person who deserved to be awarded the MC for two completely separate incidents, it could not have been given to anybody better than Colonel Donald Easten. He is a kind, modest man, whose courage and most generous spirit is an example to us all. It was just as our conversation was drawing to a close that he told me in his own very typical quiet way, of an incident that occurred during the height of the battle for Kohima. One of his men, a Lance Corporal John Harman, son of Pennington Harman, the owner of Lundy Island, decided that he would single handedly take on a Japanese machine gun post, which was about to fire on his company. Harman attacked the group of five Japanese with grenades and bayonet and was successful in killing all five, but as he returned to his company he was shot in the back from another enemy position. Despite being seriously wounded he made the last few yards, and whilst he lay dying in Donald's arms, he turned to him and said: "It was worth it Sir - I got the lot." Lance Corporal Harman's actions were those of such extreme bravery that Donald, as his company commander, proposed him for a VC, which was posthumously awarded.

I would like to take this opportunity of thanking Donald for allowing me the great honour of writing this piece. I hope in a very small way it has allowed us all to learn just a little bit more about this remarkable man.

Les Woolley

Born 7ᵗʰ October 1946

Dedicated to the late Johnny Winner - "A True and loyal East Ender"

Les Woolley is one of life's most interesting and unusual characters. If you were in trouble, you could be assured he would be there to help. Having said that, Les quite rightly does not suffer fools gladly, however I know I could put my family's life in his hands in the knowledge I would have no reason whatsoever to worry.

I met Les nearly thirty years ago when I was Joint Master and Huntsman of the Essex and Suffolk. He would be the first to admit he does not come from a normal conventional hunting background - he was born on 7ᵗʰ October 1946 in London's East End and within the sound of Bow Bells. His father was a greengrocer working the streets with a horse and cart throughout East London. He remembers that as a small boy one of the few areas to play was on the piles of bomb debris left from the Blitz. His mother died when he was nine and after what had been a tough start, life became even harder. Les is proud of many things but recognising the fact that he was born strong enough to overcome these early challenges gives him great comfort.

At an early age and not that long after his mother's death he went to work with his father. He did everything from setting up the stalls to selling the fruit and veg, as well as looking after the horse and maintaining the cart. It was around this time that Lucky, a wire haired fox terrier came on the scene, just as Les needed a bit of luck himself. His father had remarried and relations with his stepmother were at their worst. The old dog showed him great kindness and became a real mate. He would follow Les round the streets and if ever there was the slightest hint of trouble Lucky would instantly be there at his side. It was here that the great understanding and love of dogs began, which we will find out more about later.

After an unfortunate but inevitable parting of the ways with his father, Les then decided to go off hop and fruit picking in Kent and Sussex during the summer. This was his first taste of what the countryside had to offer. Working as a labourer on a building site followed, before he went on to the Watney Mann Brewery behind the notorious Blind Beggar Public House on the Mile End Road. It was still very much survival of the fittest out there and Les had to watch his back, as you never quite knew what might happen next. However, being the born survivor that he was, he coped. While working at the Brewery Les met and became the best of friends with a fellow East Ender, Johnny Winner, and they remained friends until Johnny's death. It is therefore fitting that Les has particularly asked for this piece to be dedicated to Johnny who I will be pleased to say more about a little later.

After an unfortunate but brief spell in prison, Les's life moved on and in 1967 he was happily married to Linda and nothing gave them more pleasure than their two daughters, Dawn and Nicky. In 1979, whilst they were at school in Stepney, Les noticed the girls were beginning to experience a few problems. This prompted the family to uproot and move out of the East End to Dovercourt on the Essex coast. Les soon found a job working on the railways where one of his tasks was to ensure that the platforms at Dovercourt Station were swept on a daily basis. Progressing further, he found work at the Port of Harwich. After starting at the very bottom he rose to the top of his profession and he became senior crane operator. He was responsible for loading and unloading ships coming in from all over the world.

While having a day off he came across the Essex and Suffolk hounds which had just had a good hunt and marked their fox to ground in a very large pile of roots. He was fascinated by this. Les, fresh out of the East End, had never come across an English Foxhunt before, so being Les decided to find out more. He very soon learnt that the fox, being the predator he is, was an animal whose numbers had to be kept in balance, and hunting was by far and away the best method of achieving this. Morally this suited Les. Witnessing Kevin Grey, the part time Terrier Man and countryman performing his duty most efficiently, by dispatching one of the three foxes that were in that heap of roots that day, more than likely brought Les to this thinking. He also noted that the farming community had a great affiliation with the Hunt, something he has never forgotten. As time progressed he started to help Kevin and eventually took on responsibility for the terrier work, juggling that with his official job of unloading container ships at Harwich. Les's admiration for the fox is quite clear. The animal's cunning and cleverness in avoiding being caught is something which astounds him. He also looks upon the hounds, and the terriers he has bred, as part of a whole rural pattern in which he feels greatly privileged to have been involved.

Fifteen years ago I happened to be travelling back from a British Field Sports Society meeting in London and decided to stop for a sandwich at the Blind Beggar. I was inquisitive about the history of the area as it wasn't very far away from where our immediate family had originated. I struck up a conversation with a chap at the bar who after a while asked me what I did. Slightly cautiously, I told him I was a Master of Foxhounds. "You mate, a Master of Foxhounds? God, I've got a pal that hunts, lives in 'Arwich, 'eard of it?" I replied that his friend wouldn't by any chance happen to be somebody called Les Woolley, would it? Well the old boy nearly fell of his bar stool. "How do you know my mate Les?" he said. I told him that Les had been my Terrier Man whilst I was hunting the Essex and Suffolk Hounds. For the next two hours or so the conversation never stopped and who had I been talking to for all that time? Johnny Winner.

There was an occasion fairly recently when it was brought to my attention that sadly Les had died. The Essex and Suffolk had a minute's silence for him and although they had not seen him for a while, they grieved this great character's passing. You can imagine the shock that occurred when later that year, who should appear in the Farmers bar at the Essex and Suffolk Point to Point, but Les. It was not him that had died, but I nearly did!

Hunting, the countryside and other Field Sports have made Les's life and he tells me that they have all brought him and his family endless days of happiness. Les and Linda are now proud grandparents and are teaching their grandchildren to enjoy the countryside as much as they have done throughout their lives.

Patrick Martin

The decision not to attend the funeral of a wonderful character called Charlotte Tuke came with a heavy heart. For those who did not have the pleasure of meeting her, Charlotte had for many years been a tireless worker for the British Field Sports Society and then the countryside Alliance. There would have hardly been a Point to Point in the Eastern Counties that Charlotte did not attend and it was always her way to make anybody and everybody welcome on the stand. We will miss her greatly and whether it be Burghley Horse Trials or a Point to Point on a cold wet afternoon, her absence will be sadly noticed by a very large number of our most regular supporters.

I felt that the occasion I was to attend instead was one where she too would have loved to have been, thus making my decision somewhat easier. Equally it was with the blessing of her husband Donald that I duly made my way to the Bicester country to record the activities of what is delightfully called, the Muck Heap Shoot. They were just the sort of people whose company Charlotte would have enjoyed. The day was conducted to the very highest of standards by a Keeper who knew exactly how to put a day's shooting together.

First of all though, it would be wise to find out why the shoot has this rather unusual name. It certainly isn't what you would describe as the norm and doesn't quite slip off the tongue like Blenheim, Batsford or Belvoir. The truth of the matter is that it is named after the Muck Heap at the Bicester with Whaddon Chase Hunt Kennels, and what is perhaps more unusual, the Keeper for the last twenty two years is the Huntsman Patrick Martin. There may have been many Huntsmen over the years who have had an interest in shooting but to take on the position of part time Keeper is just a little different. I have known many Keepers show a great interest in hunting, but as yet have to hear of one being a Huntsman, other than perhaps north of the Border? If there is somebody out there who is please let me know, I would be delighted to hear from you.

In this particular case, it has been fascinating to observe Patrick at work. In early September I had the pleasure of enjoying a successful morning's hunting with him at Purston. Following him back to the Kennels, we watched him feed his hounds, treat the lame ones and put them to bed after what had been a long, hard morning. Coats and boots were quickly seen to then it was away in the Land Rover to feed the pheasants. I then learnt how seriously he took his duties as a Keeper to the Muck Heap Shoot, which he also, I have to add, thoroughly enjoys.

So on 9th January we were to meet at the Shoot Captain John O Neil's farm at 9.30 am, where we were hospitably entertained by this former Master of the Bicester. We then moved off to our first drive, a small covert, but one which looked just the right sort of place to hold a goodly number of pheasants and sure enough it did. The Guns were not a team solely of hunting people by any means so this was to make the day more interesting. It wasn't many minutes after the Beaters entered the covert and pheasants started to move that a distinctive holloa rang out, informing us of the presence of one of our vulpine friends. The very fact he was there gave us great pleasure but made absolutely

Patrick Martin at the end of a hot morning with the Bicester and Whaddon Chase

no difference to the drive. After twenty minutes of swift action, fifty seven shots had been fired and twenty-four pheasants accounted for - not a bad start, with everybody getting their fair share of the shooting. This was a day when good humour was the central theme and what a pleasure it made the day. The Keeper had worked hard to ensure that everybody was part of it and this was clear to see as there was no shortage of birds throughout, with a total bag at the end of sixty-five head with another three foxes appearing, again making no difference to the drives.

As the day drew to a close, it was quite clear that we had been privileged to have taken part in a day where good spirit and good sportsmanship came together to make it such a unique occasion. It also proved that by our two sports co-operating in the way we witnessed so much had been achieved in the interests of both. The credit for this largely goes down to one man, Patrick Martin, Huntsman to the Bicester with Whaddon Chase who at the end of the season retires from both hunting the hounds and his role as game-keeper. His record for putting the countryside and our respective sports at the very forefront of working life is well renowned.

Tom Clifford
Born 3ʳᵈ June 1924

The True Hunting Farmer

Tom Clifford was born at Oddington in the Heythrop country on 3ʳᵈ June 1924 and is one of the finest examples of hunting farmers still left today. Over the years he has combined the hard physical work of livestock farming with the pleasures that hunting brings. The famous Jack Lawrence was hunting the Heythrop Hounds at the time of Tom's birth, with Colonel Brassey becoming Master the following season. Although through a lot of hard work and dedication the Heythrop is still a four day a week country, it was then in many ways very much easier for those at the sharp end to show good sport. Even with no alternative means of transportation for either horses or hounds, long hacks at the beginning and end of each day certainly did nothing to put the young Tom Clifford off this pastime.

Tom's early days of education were spent at Chipping Campden Grammar School, however his father died when he was thirteen and so most unfortunately it resulted in the family leaving Oddington to go and live in Cheltenham. This was where he was to finish his studying, at the Technical College. When he was fifteen his uncle offered him a job back at Oddington, for five shillings a week which he duly took and found himself milking twenty cows by hand, twice a day as well as taking on all the other duties that were required of a dairyman. Tom was too young to serve when war was declared on 3ʳᵈ September 1939, but he was not only fit for hard physical work but for a spot of hunting when time allowed. By a stroke of luck the legendary Percy Durno who was hunting the Heythrop at the time offered Tom his first horse, which

he kept for the duration of the War. After a while his uncle sold up and Tom went to work for Mr Bowsley at Sarsden Lodge for £1 a week before joining the Army in February 1943. During the next four years he spent a considerable amount of time out in India with his Regiment before returning back to farming at Sarsden Lodge. In August 1953, Tom married Barbara and in 1954 they decided to make a go of farming themselves so put in for the tenancy of an Oxfordshire County

Council smallholding at Shilton. It was a farm which had originally been for ex Servicemen returning from the Great War and was described by one well known farmer as the worst farm in Oxfordshire. Tom remembers it well, for a large part of it was covered in bushes and yellow daisies, otherwise known as ragwort. After six years and a considerable amount of hard work in improving the farm, Tom decided to take on a sizeable piece of land at Chadlington, which was right in the heart of the Heythrop country. Just at the very time of accepting this, his former boss Mr Boseley from Sarsden Lodge died suddenly and within two hours of his death, Tom was given the opportunity of taking on his farm. This he declined having already committed himself to the Chadlington land, where the family were to stay for the next fifteen years. However in 1975, Sarsden Lodge came up again and after beating off stiff opposition, this time Tom secured the tenancy, thus returning to the place where he had learnt so much and was where they were to spend the next thirty years.

While all this was going on, hunting with the Heythrop was still very much on the agenda. Tom broke in and hunted three and four year olds, paying a farmer's cap of two shillings and sixpence. Riding long distances to the meets was still very much on the cards as there was little transport with rationing still in place. In 1952 Percy Durno relinquished his duties of hunting the hounds to Captain Wallace who arrived from the Cotswold. The delightful way Percy handed over is still talked about today. It was the Captain who soon recognised the value of Tom Clifford, not only for being around on the hunting day but for all the other bits and pieces that he was doing for the Hunt and it wasn't long before he was rewarded by asking him to wear the hunt buttons. This was a real honour and is something he still remembers with great pride. The Captain, as we know, became well known for his organisational skills and his ability to hunt hounds most successfully in his own distinctive style. Once he was overheard saying that he was going to move off on time, but if not, preferably a little early. This particular day the hounds had met at Kingham Hill and it wasn't long before they found in Kingham Hill Covert. At 1.30 pm the hounds were at Hinchwick, having scored an eight mile point and twelve miles as they ran and Tom Clifford had been with them all the way, another highlight of his life that is still as clear in his mind today as it was all those years ago.

Tom set about farming at Sarsden Lodge in a way which only the true hunting farmer knows. A livestock man through and through, he developed beef, dairy cattle and sheep enterprises and there was also a considerable number of pigs on the place. I first met Tom thirty four years ago, when he was the same age as I am now and the whole farm stood out for being extremely tidy and was managed to perfection. I can still today see in my mind's eye why it was the farm of a proper hunting man. The coverts were expertly looked after and the hedges either laid or cut to exactly the right height for the Heythrop field to tackle when in full pursuit of the Captain and his flying bitches. More importantly there was always a healthy and strong fox population. It was therefore fitting that, not only once but on many occasions, Tom won the competition for the best fenced farm in the Heythrop country.

Tom and Barbara finally retired from farming in 2005 and went live on the outskirts of the beautiful village of Bledington, midway between Stow-on-the-Wold and Chipping Norton. Now in his nineties, Tom is still out with hounds every week accompanied by his good friend Peter Pauling and believe me they are never far from the action. It is easy for those who have experienced so much of the pleasures that hunting can give to criticise the ones who are now in the hot seat. Not him, he is full of admiration for the Masters, Staff and others who now have that responsibility and to support them to the hilt is the only way he knows. What a tremendous example he has been to very many people throughout the Heythrop country and beyond. It is a real boost to find someone who has set himself a very high standard in life and Tom you are certainly one of those.

Tom Clifford, may we wish you well and thank you for all you have given to the world of farming and foxhunting.

Peter Collins

Huntsman of the Quorn

Peter Collins, the present Huntsman of the Quorn, is a well respected member of the profession of Hunt Service and is someone you will thoroughly enjoy reading about.

All young lads have childhood ambitions about what they want to do when they grow up. Some want to be train drivers, others astronauts, but to dream as a five year old of being Huntsman of the Quorn would appear to be aiming pretty high. The fact that Peter Collins has achieved this and at fifty four years is still going strong, whilst having as much enthusiasm for the sport as when he first started, is in its own way quite remarkable. The affection he has for the hounds, and the knowledge he has of the Quorn country, is infectious to say the least and is why he is still at the very top of his profession.

Peter Collins was born into a dairy farming family on 14th December 1960. However it was their early introduction to hunting on ponies with the Cotley Harriers and the Taunton Vale Foxhounds that swayed Peter and his brother Bob away from farming towards what has been, between them, many years in Hunt Service. Whilst at Chard Comprehensive Peter was summoned to the office of the Careers Officer, a Mr Jack Handel, to discuss his future. The early signs of Peter's enthusiasm for the chase had already begun to show and Mr Handel who had a son in Hunt Service recognised it immediately. As Peter said: "He really understood my situation and as a result let me off all my exams." So he was sent to a Brigadier Driver who field mastered for the Cotley to learn the ropes in the stables. After a while the Brigadier tried to sign him up for the Kings Troop but Peter was having none of it, and made it very clear that this was not an option. He knew exactly what he wanted to do and nothing was going to change his mind, that was absolutely certain. As a result, Tony Collins ("no relation, thank God" says Peter), took him under his wing at the Heythrop where the extremely high standards of kennel management that Peter keeps in the Quorn Kennels today, are exactly as those that were drummed into him all those years ago. There was no doubt that to Tony, his hounds were his family and this really left its mark on young Peter Collins.

Peter with his son Joseph and the Quorn Hounds

After three seasons Peter was to go from one very high class establishment to another, the Fernie. Percy Durno, who had hunted the Heythrop for a number of years and also whipped in to Captain Wallace, put in a word to his son Bruce for Peter and it was here that the Leicestershire bug started to expand in the young Collins' mind. Bruce, like his father, was a wonderful hound man and hunted the Fernie with great skill and dedication, so it was the perfect place to go and further learn the trade. His next move was to somewhere completely different, the Chiddingfold, Leconfield and Cowdray as First Whipper In and Kennel Huntsman to Nigel Peel. Hunting in Sussex was a massive change to both the Heythrop and Fernie countries. It was a place where Peter could, amongst others, observe the finer arts of hunting hounds in the big Sussex woodlands. This is a different talent altogether and where patience is the most important ingredient. After going with Mr Peel to the North Cotswold, it was back to the South West to the Seavington and his first job as Huntsman. For the next nine seasons Peter put all the knowledge he had learnt from those early days into practice and showed some tremendous sport in a country which was full of supportive dairy farmers who gave the young Huntsman a great deal of encouragement. It was then back to the Chiddingfold, Leconfield and Cowdray for a while before progressing to the Portman. At this time little did he know it, but Peter's childhood ambition was becoming ever closer and after two seasons with this well known Dorset pack he was back to Leicestershire. The Quorn had been going through an unsettled patch, so it was important for Peter, as the new man on the block, to build bridges. After twelve seasons you can see quite clearly that is what he has achieved. His popularity within the country and his sense of humour stands out a mile. Like all huntsmen they have to concentrate on the job in hand, as without that the whole operation is doomed to failure. However Peter manages to combine the two rather well and always has a humorous comment ready when you meet him with his hounds flying towards you.

And so to a year in the life of Peter Collins. Peter reckons the start of the following season is the very day after he has blown home on the last. It is important to give the hounds a week off, but more than that he feels is not helpful to them. They are like children and need enough to do every day to keep them satisfied and away from quarrelling. The kennel bicycles are brought out, checked for any faults, such as loose wheels, and a week later the trusty machines are brought back into action. It is a fascinating time for a huntsman as the routine is completely different and his eye will be on next season's young hounds. These he will be observing closely and giving them all the confidence they need before it is their turn to take up the action. Once they are off couples, which will have been used during the winter whilst being walked out, they will now have a new freedom. This needs to be very carefully defined by both Huntsman and Whipper In. It is a freedom that is never discussed as it comes entirely naturally to both men how far they can let their charges go. Any further can lead to trouble and a quiet reminder may occasionally be necessary. Any reprimand must be done in a manner which does not lead to a young hound losing confidence, as otherwise all the work a Puppy Walker has put in during the early days is undone instead of being reinforced. Now is the time for Peter and his staff to take some much needed time off. It will have been a hard season as the Quorn goes out three to four days a week from the end of August until the middle of March. However, whilst holidays have to be taken, kennel routine does not change and this is vital for the happiness and contentment of a pack of hounds wherever they may be. The Quorn are lucky that their kennels are set in ninety acres of land, so during those summer months this gives Peter plenty of room for manoeuvre. The hounds and the kennels are the very hub and centre piece of any Hunt, so for whatever reason a person may hunt it is important to remember that this is the place where it all comes together and makes the day's hunting possible. It is the heart of the operation and there is no better example than here at Kirby Bellars in the middle of Leicestershire.

As the spring turns to summer there are plenty of duties to perform and these fit neatly into a Huntsman's year. Whilst bringing on the young hounds that were born in the spring of the previous year more will be born and will need a great deal of care and attention. This is another part of Peter's everyday life and one he takes very seriously. Twelve to fifteen couple is the ideal number for the Quorn and whilst in days gone past they hunted a dog pack and a bitch pack, more often nowadays they are mixed as there are not quite the numbers of hounds being bred as there were. The months quickly roll by and during this time Peter Collins, his bicycle and the hounds will be covering much of the Leicestershire countryside in their summer keep fit campaign. Calls to outlying farms will be made as well as to others who possibly are unable to get out and about as much as they would like. They may be to a previous Puppy Walker or someone else who has been involved in one way or another over the years. It matters not, the pleasure it can give to see the Quorn Hounds in this case on their doorstep is immense as Peter knows only too well. On such a visit when a hound suddenly recognises its old walker and decides to leap into their arms, he knows something is working pretty well.

Preparations and practice for the Puppy Show, as well as taking his young ones out to walk, have to be fitted into Peter's busy summer schedule. Also included are the hound parades at local shows, the hound shows themselves and most importantly preparing the country for the coming season. Once holidays are taken there is little rest for him and his staff. However all this is undertaken with the greatest good humour for which Peter is well known and respected. The Puppy Show is a large event for the Quorn and a good opportunity for the locals and those from far and wide to come to the Kennels and cast their eyes not only over the young hounds but the old stagers who have worked so hard over the past seasons. These hounds are fairly orthodox in most of their breeding, however surprisingly there is a considerable influence of French blood as well as some wolf in them. The fine detail of such an experiment is fascinating to say the least and is well worth delving into.

Hunting the Quorn hounds is a mixture of many different balances. Knowing and trusting your hounds and the horse you are riding is where the golden thread comes into play and it all starts from there. Without it one might as well not bother and become a civil servant or something equally uninteresting. Peter has just the rapport to make it work and I would certainly trust his ability in this direction perhaps more than I would than if he were in local government. With his wife Lorna being Stud Groom, this helps to ensure harmony between stables and kennels and allows Peter to enjoy what he loves most, entering his young hounds and watching them gaining confidence as the season progresses. This is all absorbing, watching them in their second season. Seeing them really beginning to excel is his reward for all the work he has put into them. It is at this stage he will be looking at who has potential to use as stallion hounds and from which bitches to breed.

From 1st November the chips are down for Peter and doesn't he know it. The last two seasons have been extremely bad scenting and made life tough for both him and his beloved hounds. However, it would seem that with the gift he has of managing to keep the tambourine a-rolling with a natural smile on his face and twinkle in his eye, Peter ensures all about him are kept rather well amused. This is of course helped by the Quorn country being made easily crossable by those who take charge of the fencing and covert maintenance throughout the season.

So we have to ask this son of a West country dairy farmer, who has a passion for fast motorbikes and has achieved his ambition to hunt the Quorn hounds, what advice would he have for those young professionals of today who are keen to achieve their dream? "Keep smiling" he says, and "always raise your hat to whoever he or she may be." Peter Collins would not have changed anything in his life and observing him on the hunting field and listening to the enthusiasm that so clearly still exists, my advice to anybody wanting to going into Hunt Service would be to take a leaf out of Peter Collins' book. With young Joe, Peter's son coming along and looking as though he may have the same enthusiasm for the chase as his father, there just could be another huntsman of the Quorn in the making here. Well done Peter.

John Stride

Born 28ᵗʰ October 1949

On 2ⁿᵈ June 1100, whilst hunting deer in the New Forest, King William II, or William Rufus as he was better known, was killed by an arrow from Sir William Tyrell's bow. For the next eight hundred and ninety seven years the hunting of the Fallow Deer in one form or another continued to take place every year right up until 26ᵗʰ March 1997. This is when urban pressures culminated together and became the cause of the New Forest Buckhounds having their last day's hunting. It was not only a truly sad occasion, but also with their passing went a deep knowledge and understanding of the Fallow Deer and most importantly their welfare.

A statement was made on their disbandment on 28ᵗʰ July of that year. However the one person who probably knew more about the deer then and more than likely still does till this day, is their former huntsman John Stride. Before 1997 the Buckhounds had been an integral part of forest life for generations of New Foresters. However the pressure that was beginning to build from middle class suburban thinking on many of the traditions of the forest was beginning to take its toll. The changes witnessed over the years have been phenomenal and as many have found out, not been for the better. It is therefore extremely sad but fitting, as John was the last man to have hunted the fallow buck in the United Kingdom, that we should hear his life story, which is truly fascinating.

Born into a New Forest family in Lyndhurst on 28ᵗʰ October 1949, John was brought up at Blackwater Farm on the southern side of the forest, between Denny Lodge and Beaulieu Road Station, where his parents still live today. At seven years old however, he was moved back to Lyndhurst to live with his grandparents for schooling purposes, as he was the only child out there in the wilds. The authorities felt they couldn't justify the cost of sending a taxi all that way to take him backwards and forwards to school, so that was the only way the problem could be resolved. Once his brother and sister reached school age, John was allowed to return home.

During these early days his father and mother would have taught him all the different aspects that make the New Forest such an interesting place to live and work. He would have learnt what makes it tick on a day to day basis throughout the year and to respect the different seasons. Probably more information would have been absorbed during the holidays than there ever was at school and being from a family that had been there for several generations, this would have hardly been surprising. Many an hour would also be spent on an autumn evening watching the deer and maybe just a day or two before the hounds were in the area, they would be observed a little closer to see if there was a warrantable buck amongst them. This is what is called harbouring and it is all about finding the right animal which is at the right age and maturity to be taken if at all possible. The New Forest has for a long time been a place where the general public have had open access so this makes

the use of a high powered rifle very much more dangerous, thus the use of hounds was not only a viable alternative, but was very much safer.

John's first memory of the Buckhounds came when his father had been asked to harbour a buck for the Monday. It was early autumn and he knew where there

John Stride (left) with Chris Compton MBH and New Forest Keeper Graham Wilson

was an old apple tree in the middle of Denny Wood, which the deer liked to visit at that time of year. In fact so much so, they were like bees round a honey pot. Off John and he set to see what they could find and after a considerable time quietly watching and observing, just before darkness fell they picked out a buck that ideally needed taking out before winter set in. He was past his best and not in good condition.

His father would report back to the huntsman Stan Read at the Meet the next morning of the possible whereabouts of the harboured buck and the rest of the herd. All things being equal they should be lying up fairly close by, but the slightest bit of disturbance during the night could have meant they were long gone. After checking again as the sun rose, it was then over to Stan and the Tufters to do the rest. This is where the exact science kicks in, for he might be in amongst a herd of up to a hundred others and it is the job of those few couple of old stagers to split him off from the rest of the herd. Once he was well away from them the pack would be laid on and the hunt would commence. On this occasion the buck decided very promptly that he was not going far and that he would visit the Stride family garden. More than likely he had been there before with the intention of eating their vegetables. However he came face to face with the seven year old John walking up the path. Narrowly avoiding each other he decided to take up residence in the pig sty where he was promptly dispatched.

As John continued to grow up he remembers the Masters traditionally came round at Christmas and thanked the Keepers and their families for their help and support during the season. They would bring a bottle of whisky for the husband and there would always be something for the wife. It helped tremendously in cementing good relations with those who lived and worked in the forest. This may have been just a small act which originated from the time when Sir George Thursby, and latterly the Sir Dudley Forwoods, were Masters, but undoubtedly it was greatly appreciated.

John's Mother was very keen on New Forest ponies and they also became very much part of his upbringing, so much so that when the Beagles met locally he would make sure there was one handy for him to leap on. Therefore he could go and enjoy the afternoon's activities. As well as John's family being enthusiastic supporters of the Buckhounds and the Beagles this extended to the Foxhounds whose Kennels are still at Lyndhurst.

In 1963 Sir Newton Rycroft was elected their Master and it wasn't going to be very long before he really left his mark on John and his brother Richard, as these two examples will clearly demonstrate. His hound control was quite something to be believed. On one occasion his hounds had marked a fox to ground on a bank side. He walked across to them and quietly collecting them said: "Come on boys and girls, now you come with me." He took them to the opposite bank and patiently asked them to stay there whilst he went off to investigate further. Not a hound put a foot out of place and a whip was never used. At the New Forest Show at New Park, he took them to one end of the ring and left them there. He would then walk to the far side and call individual hounds out to go to him, and they did, with no deviation whatsoever. Sir Newton was a renowned naturalist and there was hardly anything he didn't know about the New Forest. His empathy and knowledge of birds, as well as the deer, fox and badger populations that occupied this large area, was a great example of a true hunting man's interest in the conservation of many different species. It was therefore a great pity that those who tried so hard to strip the Forest of its traditional activities didn't take more notice of this kind and most intelligent man. What a privilege it must have been for the Stride Brothers to have learnt so much from him.

This they did to fine example with Richard taking up a position at the Foxhound Kennels and John going from working with the Forestry Commission to whip in to the Buckhounds from 1966 to 1968 before returning back to the Commission. In the early '70s Mr. Donald Egremont put John on to whip in to Stan Read before he was offered the position to hunt the hounds in 1989. During John's first few seasons Sir Newton would very often turn up at the Kennels having as a point of principle always sought the Master's permission first. He was fascinated to hear about how they had been getting on and appeared to be as keen on the breeding of their hounds as he was his own. It was his understanding of the deer and the mutual interest he shared with John of the New Forest that helped enormously in John's first few seasons.

As a huntsman there were numerous times John would have to think hard and quick as to what his hunted buck might do next. However whilst whipping in to Stan Read, he recollects hounds had run into a gorse brake and Stan said to him: "Now stand quietly and watch and see what happens." With that he noticed the buck going in and out of the gorse pushing up the prickets (young bucks) with his antlers. Not only did he do this but he kept them moving along, when suddenly he turned and jumped three or four of them and then clapped down like a hare. From what we believe this behaviour is very much a trait of the Fallow Deer. On another occasion the hounds had run down to Dockens Water and had lost their buck. John was one side and Stan the other and after much searching, out of the corner of his eye, John noticed the very tip of a nose and the top of his antlers showing above the water. Both these incidents highlight the intelligence of the hunted animal and the respect man should have for him.

One of the best hunts in John's career came again when he was whipping in, this time from a Meet at Denny, that great stronghold for the deer. Unusually the tufters were not required as Johnny Francombe had harboured two bucks in Pond Head. One was soon split away and hounds quickly settled down to run well over the Beaulieu road to Longwater where they turned and pushed on across to Matley Wood. From here they went over the main road without a check into Denny New past Ranmoor Cottage to the Bournemouth to Lymington road which they crossed into New Park. Passing the Kennels they went on as hard as they could to Queen Mead Field to the Bournemouth Brockenhurst road where the buck jumped the new fencing into Knightmoor Enclosure and then to Woosons Hill. Here the buck decided to make his point for Minstead Manor by crossing the Bolderwood Road and going through Holm Hill Enclosure and Acres Down before reaching his destination where he was given best. Without any doubt this was a very tough fallow buck, who found himself greatly admired by all who were out that day. Later that evening, he was observed cooling himself off in the ford on the Minstead Road, seemingly totally unscathed and unfazed by the whole performance.

Since 1854 the New Forest Buckhounds were served by Masters who could not have been more dedicated to the Fallow Deer. Thursby, Forwood, Daresbury, Buchanan Jardine and latterly Millar, Compton, Marshall, and there are many more who could be mentioned, played a most valuable and important role in the survival of the species. Without their expertise and that of their Huntsmen over the years, it is more than likely the Fallow Deer of the New Forest would not be in such a strong position as they are today.

John, you come from a very old and respected Forest family. You are the last man in Great Britain today to have hunted the Fallow Buck. Be proud of a job very well done in what were extremely difficult times for you and your hounds. We salute you and all your colleagues, be they Keepers, Harbourers or your loyal Supporters for your most courageous efforts. Without this form of dedication some of the further incidents that occurred whilst John was Huntsman would not have been witnessed. I am therefore indebted to Mrs Chris Compton who was Master right up until the end and served the Hunt for ten seasons for letting me have these intriguing pieces.

For those who hunted at that particular time in the New Forest, either with the Buckhounds or the Foxhounds, many would never have known there was a large herd of wild fallow deer that lived around the Kennels in New Park. Very often hounds would be walked out past them and would have learnt not to go near them. There were numerous very experienced hound men who thought this would have not have been possible, but this was a true fact. On one memorable day in the '90s John was hunting the hounds, and they had hunted their buck well when he decided to come down into New Park and join the herd. It was at this exact point that every hound stopped absolutely dead in its tracks. A keeper then came and carefully walked the buck out of the herd and the hounds were taken round and laid on his line again and away they went. Quite a remarkable piece of hound control to say the least and just may have come from John quietly observing Sir Newton Rycroft in his younger days.

On another occasion two followers were sitting quietly on their horses waiting for a large herd of Red Deer to cross the ride in front of them. The deer were in no hurry and hounds could be heard hunting towards them and at the time were not far away. Then suddenly one of the riders seemed to notice steam coming from the middle of the herd. On closer inspection there was the hunted buck right amongst the Reds, just meandering along at their pace.

It was very often the case that during a hunt the buck would run to a herd of does and it was extraordinary to see them pushing the male out as if to tell him he was not welcome there bringing danger to them and their offspring.

Lastly, as the very subject of this book is honouring the living and the departed, it would be very remiss of me not to mention this rather strange but moving incident which tells us even more that these incidents after a death are not just restricted to foxes. In 'Final Curtain' we come across the unusual behaviour of the Red Deer on Exmoor after Frank Dallyn, the harbourer to the Devon and Somerset Staghounds, died. We now have the Fallow Deer of the New Forest behaving in a rather peculiar fashion exactly a year after the death of David Marshall, one of the last Masters of the Buckhounds. David was a giant of a man in size and heart. He was born and grew up in the depth of London's East End not knowing what his future would be. He purchased a property in the New Forest and started riding with his daughter Tina. They became subscribers to the Buckhounds and, always one to help, David joined the Mastership in 1988 becoming much loved by both followers and forest folk alike. Tina went on to hunt the New Forest Beagles for many years.

After the Buckhounds had disbanded David hunted with the Quantock Staghounds and while out with them one day with Chris Compton he suddenly died. David was buried at Burley in the heart of the Forest. On the first anniversary of his death the Vicar reported that the deer were invading the churchyard and taking flowers from the graves. After much investigation it transpired that the only two that were being vandalised were David's and another great supporter of the New Forest Buckhounds.

Here's to Jim and the Burton Hunt!

Jim Lang was born on 26th July 1939 at Redruth Hospital in Cornwall and ever since that eventful day, many of us at some point will have realised that the world without Jimmy Lang would indeed be a very dull place.

Jim came from a family with traditional Cornish roots, his father Sam being Stockman to Major John Williams, who was Master of the Four Burrow and owned the Scorrier Estate, close to Truro. Jim's mother Dorothy already had one son Ken, however she sadly died three years after Jim was born whilst giving birth to their

Jim and his well known smile

sister Christine. It soon became apparent that Mr Lang senior was most fortunate to possess a deep knowledge of the equine world and this assisted him greatly when being promoted to Stud Groom to the Williams' family. The position of turning out the ten hunt horses throughout the season for the Hunt Staff and the family was one he took extremely seriously. One of Jim's earliest memories as a little boy was of leaning over the garden gate watching the hounds hacking home from hunting in the dusk and Mr Percival Williams, the Major's father, calling out to him that they had caught one that day.

Although Jim was only two months old when War was declared with Germany, the latter part of it was something he has vivid memories of, as the Germans repeatedly tried to bomb the oil terminal at nearby Falmouth. There was a considerable number of Americans in Cornwall then who were preparing for the D Day Landings. They were based in the big country houses in the area, and when they left they gave away all their spare food to the villagers, and with strict rationing in place, this was more than welcome. Jim being Jim also obtained the army cat which then lived with the family for many years afterwards. Hunting managed to continue, but on a much reduced basis and Jim remembers one morning when the hounds had caught a fox, he found himself submerged by the whole pack of Four Burrow Hounds and was told by Mr Percival that he would have to get used to this. Well if anyone was to find himself getting used to it, Jim was certainly the right candidate.

At the age of fifteen and a half he went into the stables under his father and was allowed to have the odd day whipping in. It was on these occasions that the Master would take Jim and they would sit quietly on a covert side and wait for the foxes to come towards them. After a while, having seen perhaps two or three he would ask Jim which he thought was the hunted one, and more often than not, Jim would have the right answer. It not only earned him praise but taught him a great deal about the fox. This arrangement continued until the time came when Jim was meant to go off and do his National Service. Good luck however intervened as it was about the time the tenth Duke of Beaufort came to stay at Scorrier with Mr Percival and on seeing Jim working with the cattle one day, put his head over the door and told Jim that he had heard he was going off to do his National Service and asked Jim if he really wanted to go? The reply came, "Well, not really, Your Grace." The Duke left saying that he would see what he could do. Time went on and about ten days before he was due to leave, the green papers of exemption arrived. They had not taken into consideration that hunting was a service to the agricultural community and that people were going to be much needed in this profession. So Jim stayed at Scorrier for the next few years gaining more experience of the Four Burrow Hounds which at the time were being hunted by Mr John Williams. He too, like his father, was somebody who had numerous contacts throughout the hunting world which were in time to turn out in Jim's favour.

It was in the early '60s when one of these contacts, a Captain Dermot Kelly, was looking for a Second Whipper In to assist him in his new position as Master and Huntsman of the Meynell. Jim was summoned to London for an interview which took place at the unusual venue of the Cavalry Club. He arrived on time and was described to me by Mr Kelly as resembling a frightened rabbit. However all went well and the frightened rabbit secured the job. Little did either of them know at the time, but this was to be Jim's lucky break and was very much going to be the making of him. However before he made his way back to Cornwall that day, Mr Kelly sent him off on a tour of London, taking in such places as Green Park and Buckingham Palace, where he remembers watching the Changing of the Guard. This was quite an eye opener for a young Cornish lad who was in London for the first time and on his own.

So a few months later he was off to Derbyshire and Jim was soon to find out just how different to Cornwall it was. The First Whipper In and KH at the time was the late John Cooke (Cookie) who went on to hunt the Wilton and was followed by another great character, also now recently deceased, the late Johnny O' Shea who after a while took the opportunity to go and hunt the Cheshire which he did most successfully for twenty-five seasons. Working for Mr Kelly was never dull but there was an important aspect one had to take into consideration whilst working for him, and that was to look sharp, keep one's wits about one at all times and be able to see something happening before it actually did. A sense of humour was also an important addition to the list of these abilities, and there was no shortage of that around in Derbyshire at the time, with John Cooke, Johnny O'Shea, Jim and the Boss all possessing it in rather large quantities.

On one occasion they were hunting from the Red Lion at Keddleston. It was snowing, sleeting, blowing as well as raining as they hacked on to draw, so Jim thought it would be wise to turn his collar up against the elements. The next moment there was a roar from Mr Kelly who had noticed Jim committing the offence. He told him in no uncertain terms that he was fired and a disgrace to Hunt Service. He then went on to ask who the hell did

he think he was and Jim in his own amusing way soon had the upper hand of the situation by replying very politely, "I am someone from a far warmer climate than this, Sir." Not many days afterwards, they were trotting on to a Meet on a beautiful frosty morning, when Jim announced to the boss, "Isn't it a beautiful morning, Sir, a proper winter wonderland, we don't get frost like this in Cornwall you know." The reply from Mr Kelly came back instantly telling him to shut up boy, for God's

Jim Lang (right) with his former Boss Dermot Kelly

sake and to concentrate on what he was doing! On another occasion Jim rather mistakenly announced after a rather good hunt that he had jumped thirty two fences. He hadn't realised that he had been overheard, when suddenly a voice came from nowhere telling him very sharply that he was not there to enjoy himself and that he had got a b.......... job to do!

Well Jim must have put his mind to what he was doing and although this did not stop him being fired on numerous occasions, both he and Mr Kelly were clearly at the beginning of building up a most healthy respect for each other. This was something I was fortunate enough to witness, over fifty years later when Jim and I were both asked by Mr Kelly to go down to Gloucestershire and have lunch with him. Arriving at noon, the next three hours or so were spent with the two of them reminiscing about the great days they had enjoyed, and on our return journey, Jim turned to me and said, "You know Mr Barclay, it was Mr Kelly that took me on from being a keen young Cornish lad with a little experience and turned me into a true professional."

It was after another particularly good day when they had returned to the Kennels, Mr Kelly took Jim on one side and told him that he had to be at the Quorn Kennels for nine o'clock sharp on the Friday morning. It may have taken just a minute or two for the penny to drop, but the reason soon became clear, and that was because the Quorn were looking for a Second Whipper In and it was Jim's turn to be interviewed for the post by Jack Littleworth, their well respected Huntsman.

This was the day that Jim really had to show just how good he was and that he was worthy of the position, but he had only one horse. The Meet was at Scraptoft and the hounds ran well all morning, and as they called a halt at Second Horses he hoped that he had done enough to please Mr Littleworth. Before he was to find out his fate, something was to happen to Jim, which he least expected. As he was handing over his horse, a large Rolls Royce drew up beside him. In the back seat sat the late Alan Whicker who was out filming the documentary about the Quorn, "Death in the Morning." Jim was soon whisked up, put in the back of the car and plied with a glass of whisky. He was asked numerous questions about what was going to happen to him next, so Jim explained the process of employment to Mr Whicker and how much he wanted to secure the job.

This he duly did, the rest is history and on 1st May 1964 he joined Jack Littleworth and his First Whipper In, Michael Farrin. His Meynell days had come to an end and those at the Quorn were about to begin, however the days with Mr Kelly will be remembered for all the right reasons. From the beginning, Jim was taught the single most important aspect about becoming a good Whipper In, and that was to be able to count hounds, and count them quickly. The one who can do this is invaluable to his Huntsman at any time, but especially nowadays as Jim explains, "The roads are a nightmare and are becoming ever busier all the time."

Jim will never forget his experience of hunting with the Quorn, with two horses on Mondays and Fridays it was a unique insight into hunting in the Shires and he felt privileged to be a part of it. He remembers the Quorn for being a lovely pack of hounds and Jack Littleworth, a top class huntsman, whose horses went extremely well for him, crossing the Quorn country as they did with tremendous ease. In the Kennels he was always cheerful and whistling, something perhaps that was to rub off on his young Second Whipper in. Jim and Michael were treated like family and were always given breakfast every morning. This led to the two Whippers In forging a great friendship which was to last right up to the time of Michael's untimely death in 2006. What they got up to heaven only knows, but I believe it was all in good humour. Many great days were enjoyed and are now still vivid in Jim's memories. One in particular was a Meet at the Remount Depot at Melton Mowbray when there was a field of over three hundred out. The three of them certainly had to look sharp that day.

Jim and his great pal John Goode former Huntsman of the Brocklesby

Time came to move on and early in 1966 Jim went on interview for the First Whipper In's job at the Burton. The Meet was at East Barkwith and happened to be one of the wettest days they had experienced all season. However hounds flew and gave a really good account of themselves, running right out into the South Wold country and back into their own. Whilst they were boxing up at the end of the day, Master, Mr Arthur Lockwood, turned to Jim and his then amateur Whipper In Stephen Fieldsend and said, "It is not always as wet as this here, is it Stephen?" Quick as a shot Stephen, who was later to become Joint Master, replied "It is only as wet as this in winter Sir!"

Jim secured the position at the Burton, whilst Michael Farrin stayed on as First Whipper In at the Quorn. In May 1968 Michael was promoted to Huntsman after the early retirement of Jack Littleworth due to ill health. By this time Jim had made his move across to Lincolnshire, a most unusual change for someone who many might have thought was destined to become Huntsman to one of the Shire Packs. However unusual it was there were three reasons for it, the first being Mr Arthur, who knew instinctively that he had the right man for the job and made that very clear to Jim. The second reason was the majority of the bigger jobs were looking for married men and Jim hadn't quite got that far, and the third being the most important to Jim was the appeal of hounds hunting across the large arable fields of the Eastern Counties. For him this was far greater than what the galloping grasslands of Leicestershire had to offer. Most of the time he could see what the hounds were up to and this was going to be more and more important to him. After whipping in to Jack King for just one season, Jim was offered the position of Huntsman for the 1967/'68 season which he was delighted to take and here he stayed at the Burton until his well deserved retirement in 2006.

The skill of hunting the fox in a plough country is a fine art, and Jim developed a real knack for this. To be able to observe the many different aspects that make up a day without being pushed by large numbers of thrusters was to him the biggest advantage. It also taught him how to read what a fox might do next. This often gave him the opportunity to pull off long hunts that would hardly ever have been possible in hard riding Leicestershire. However, his first season one can only say was a total disaster. It started with his best hound being killed out on hound exercise when it was kicked by the amateur Whipper In's horse. Then shortly after the Opening Meet a serious outbreak of Foot and Mouth was declared in the Eastern Counties. This caused all hunting in the Burton country and elsewhere to cease. The following year got off to a better start with the team being strengthened by Mr Arthur appointing Stephen Fieldsend as his Joint Master. Stephen farmed in the Aisthorpe, Scampton area and was and still is a committed foxhunter, as are the whole family, with Richard, his son, now Chairman. Stephen served a five year term and has many great memories of hunting with Jim. On his retirement from the Mastership he was asked by Mr Arthur if he wouldn't mind just doing a spot of field mastering from time to time. Actually he ended up taking on the job for the next ten years, such were the persuasive powers of his Joint Master. The hounds at this time had started to gel as Jim wanted them, and sport was continuing to improve with the long hunts in the open beginning to materialise.

None of this happens by luck alone, and it is not only down to what a Huntsman does in the Kennels nor on a hunting day. To produce really good sport the organisation and planning of the hunting country is a must and to this extent there was no one better at it than Mr Arthur, for whom Jim has tremendous respect and admiration. Mr Arthur's father was Master for six seasons from 1948. He was renowned for his meticulous planning, knowing every farmer throughout the Burton country and where they could or couldn't go. After a while Jim took on the responsibility of looking after the smaller farmers and the keepers. He would report back to the boss the night before hunting and if there was a problem with access to a certain area due to shooting, very often it would lead to the shoot changing their plans, not the Burton Hunt. As Jim says, for the relationship between Master and Huntsman to work, "You have to be on the same wave length" and no truer words have been uttered. He added: "It was important to know when to ask and when not to ask." This is a vital point and one where mutual respect very much comes to the fore.

The continuity of the Lockwood family has played a crucial role in the fortunes of the Burton Hunt since Mr Bill Lockwood took on the Mastership. Their kindly, supportive influence over hunting not only in their own country but nationwide has been one of the most outstanding contributions to our sport. No family deserves more credit for all they have achieved. With Jim as Huntsman to Mr Arthur and latterly Mr John, they oversaw a pack of hounds that has continued to improve. Whilst there were difficult challenges that had to be faced when the majority of the Burton pack was lost due to strychnine poisoning and then more hounds were lost after they consumed infected flesh, support from hunts around the country for this most respected family ensured it wasn't long before they were up and running again. It was something that was bound to have left its mark on the Hunt overall as all the most valuable breeding lines had now gone, but as time progressed they returned to their old form producing long hunts across the Lincolnshire plough, as well as starting to win prizes again at the major Hound Shows across the land. Although times had no doubt been difficult, the Burton was not going to be down for long and was soon climbing once more to the top of the tree, which is where they are today.

Despite having to deal with the horrific effects of the Hunting Act of 2005, Jim carried on hunting hounds with great success right up to his retirement in 2006. It was hard to believe on his last day at Hackthorn that he was in his forty-second season with the Burton, nor that he was beginning to suffer from a life threatening disease. He was crossing the country as well as ever with the same old smile that goes with the character of this man, but the time had come when a very tough decision had to be made. Jim was keen for his position to be filled by his former Whipper In, Neil Burton, who had been hunting the Glamorgan Hounds most successfully for

the previous twelve seasons. Jim was going to be greatly missed but Neil was more than capable of successfully succeeding the great man.

After several operations Jim returned to good health. This was largely down to his overall fitness and it wasn't long before he was out again on his old grey horse, watching and observing from further afield. The hounds settled for Neil and whilst it may have been

Arthur Lockwood hunting with the Burton

Photograph by Jim Meads

somewhat hard to have his old boss looking on, results began to speak for themselves. Neil had been lucky and had a good upbringing in Hunt Service, starting in the Kennels at the South Wold with Johnny Cooke before progressing to the East Sussex and Romney Marsh, the Holderness and the South Notts before whipping in at the Burton and then hunting the Glamorgan. With the help of William Deakin at the Holderness, he developed a sharp eye for a fox which may have been quietly tickling on way in front of hounds. All this stood him in good stead and has helped him develop his own style, which he believes Jim wanted him to do. So with Jim's breeding of the Burton Hounds left intact, this is what Neil has unquestionably achieved.

Hunting has gone through extremely tough times over the last ten years or so, however it is the strength of community that exists at the Burton as elsewhere which keeps us all united. The Lockwood family along with their Joint Masters have been custodians of the hounds since 1948 and they have set a wonderful example of encouraging each and every section of society into the fold. This is what is necessary to make a hunt work properly, with every individual having a role to play.

So before we finish let us consider for a moment how fortunate the Burton has been to have had Jim Lang and his smiling happy face at the helm for over forty years. Now they have Neil Burton who is doing his best to make every success of hunting and breeding the hounds. Like many he has a great belief in the young, encouraging them to become involved and in his case not only with the Hunt but with what he sees as his hounds. This has become abundantly clear during his time at the Burton and on the very last day of the 2014/2015 season he handed his hunting horn over to his young Whipper In, Charlie Thomas, who is temporarily leaving Hunt Service to go farming. What a most generous and encouraging gesture.

So here's to Jim Lang for having been a fine example of a Huntsman with great character and dedication, Neil who has the future in the forefront of his mind and the Burton Hunt for showing us all the right path to take.

THE STABLE YARD IS SILENT

The Stable yard is now silent, no old friends ears, twitching over the bars,

Where have they gone? They have gone to Europe to fight a war,

Will they be back to graze the summer pastures green?

Will they be back to see the autumn mist and hear hounds running?

Will they be back to enjoy the fifty minutes across the grass?

They and their masters have gone to defend our freedom,

In mud and wire they toil, no end in sight,

But the thought of hounds running and their cry deep in their veins

Makes our horse and human friends dream, dream of

A cold winter's night, hacking homewards with the moon up high.

This dreadful battle must soon be over, no more dust, no more artillery fire,

The guns shall fall silent, then it's back across the sea to the land we love,

When the time will come again, to be harnessed to the plough

Or saddled fit and ready for a day with the hounds.

A hundred years hence, let us just spare a thought,

Hounds still running and running hard they are across the Vale below,

Imagine the pleasures of leaping that bullfinch clear and straight.

We can see you now! We can see you clearly from heaven above.

For we are at peace, peace in the knowledge as the fight to us came,

We took it on and gave it our best,

To find a future, sadly we were not to see,

Time though is now for those with younger spirit to go and play their part.

As the morning sun rises above the silver mist,

We hear a pack of foxhounds flying and a holloa that chills the spine

Charlie has slipped from the covert and quickly gone away,

Then like shadows from the past,

Before our very eyes, is a field of swift and gallant horses, galloping on the turf!

The guns of war are silent, our battles fought, our battles won,

The stables are full once more, with spirits old and spirits new,

Ears twitching again over stable bars, as always was their way,

And those dear hounds are singing, with heads held proudly high

And a note in their voice that says, we are here, and here we are to stay.

THE FINAL CURTAIN?

'An Old Friend' passes over my family graves

When the final curtain falls on our lives, is it really the very end of our existence? Perhaps there is another side to the argument and we should stand back for a minute or so and think? Over the years I have had the great privilege to meet, work and spend valuable time with some truly wonderful people, many of whom are still here today but also with others who have sadly gone on to another place and are now at rest.

It is quite something to be able to share with you some experiences that occurred not only to me after a death, but to friends who have witnessed similar instances of unusual behaviour from our many species. These are not unique, but have had a very moving effect on those of us who have been there and seen them for ourselves. They encourage us to consider our own mortality and think about what is going to come to us when we meet our final fence. All these pieces are true, so imagine as the final curtain drops when you are next at the theatre or a musical performance, is there going to be an encore that evening or will it all just come to an abrupt halt? No one knows the answer, that is for sure. Except to say if the performance has been as you would expect, there more than likely will be! Think about this as these stories are retold. Hopefully they will intrigue you.

James Barclay

Captain Charles Geoffrey Edward Barclay
13th August 1919 – 5th July 2002

The father of all four younger Barclays, Charles Geoffrey Edward, was born at Brent Pelham in the heart of the Puckeridge country on 13th August 1919. Known fondly by his many friends as Charlie and in later years as the Captain, his childhood was spent with his younger brother Billy and sister Pamela hunting with the Puckeridge, where his father and grandfather had been Joint Masters for some considerable time. He was educated at Eton, where he whipped in to Ronnie Wallace before going on to study agriculture at Cambridge and taking on the Mastership of the Trinity Foot Beagles. Ronnie then progressed to Oxford where he became Master of the Christchurch College Beagles.

Father's brother Billy joined the Navy and was tragically lost at sea during the Russian Convoys. Father served with the North Somerset Yeomanry from 1939 before being demobbed in 1946. During active service he met many people who remained long lasting friends but they also played an important part in the rest of his life.

His wartime career saw him serving in various different parts of the world, which included Palestine, Syria, the Western Desert, Greece, Sicily, Italy, France, Belgium, Holland and Germany. Whilst guarding the Athens telephone exchange with the late Captain John Foster, a former Master of the Wheatland, he was shot in the legs by the Greeks. Much to his amusement the shrapnel would often set off airport security systems, but once he had explained the situation he was allowed to pass through unhindered. His war years ended with him being mentioned in dispatches.

Gone Away

And so Old Friend you have now slipped away
Past the dark covert – where the stream runs grey,
Through mud and mire, heavy plough no more
Shall you now toil as you toiled before.
Quick as a flash you heard the view holloa.
Answered the Call and there old friend you go.
What's that they say? "I think she's gone to ground"
Ah no she is upward bound
Yonder she goes where the sun shines high
If we ride straight, perhaps you too and I
May cross the final steep-banked awful brook
To find the peace for which we look.
Goodbye for now, but this is not the end.
Just till we meet again, all is well old Friend

"Peccavi"

(left to right) Grandfather, Father and Great Grandfather
with Puckeridge President (1948)

Returning home after what had been an eventful war he took over the family farm at Brent Pelham, developing a large flock of Suffolk sheep and latterly a herd of 200 Friesian milking cows. The Puckeridge Hounds, which hunt a very heavy, cold scenting plough country, also became an institution under his Mastership and that of our forebears. They were originally a pure English pack, but after his father's death in 1962 he skilfully managed to include more Beaufort and Heythrop blood into them, thus improving their size. His ability to hunt a fox on the most difficult day was remarkable and he possessed a wonderful knack of keeping the tambourine a-rolling. He could almost read what his quarry was going to do next, probably before it knew itself. There were many times you would wonder why he would be casting in a particular direction, when suddenly his hounds would hit off the line and away they would go. In his last few years he would not always be with them during a flying hunt, but you could bet that as soon as the hounds had either caught their fox, marked it to ground or somehow they needed help, he would be there, as if appearing from nowhere.

In his latter days father followed in his Discovery, normally driven by one of the ever loyal Australian or New Zealand carers who would have been taught to have as sharp an eye for a fox as he did. On one occasion he was sitting waiting as his hounds drew a thick covert towards him. His favourite old Doghound Dragon sat there accompanying him. This was allowed as he too was becoming an old man. Suddenly a fox appeared right in front of the pair of them. Encouraged in no uncertain terms by the Boss, Dragon duly took off, forgetting his age and swiftly despatched the fox. He then proceeded to try and bring it back for father to inspect.

As the end drew near father was confined to bed downstairs. One morning he asked for his hounds to be brought to him as he had not seen them for a while. Luke Neil his Joint Master brought them down from the Kennels to the front garden and then straight into his room. Where did Dragon go? Directly to his bed, front feet up, and after making a fuss of father, tried to devour the toy fox which was immediately above his head.

A few months later Father died peacefully at home on 5th July 2002. Both his Funeral and Memorial Service were attended by a large number of family and friends. Later that evening we all gathered to say our last goodbyes, with Dragon and my terrier Murphy in attendance. As we blew gone away and then home, there was Dragon curled up in front of the grave with his head held high and Murphy singing his heart out.

Normally the Puckeridge hounds would start hunting from the Kennels at Brent Pelham towards the end of August. This particular year was different as they were needed to go and sort out some troublesome foxes on the flatlands out towards Cambridge. They got there at 6.30 am only to find it was impossible to hunt due to thick fog which never cleared all morning. After waiting for a while it was decided to return home and go on hound exercise. Trotting down the road from the kennels for half a mile they turned off on to a farm track and standing there in the mist and within two hundred and fifty yards of the road, sat a very large old fox. Hounds soon winded him and they were gone. My sister realised where he was going. He went straight through the Hall Wood, across the Park and into father's vegetable garden, over the road and into the Churchyard, just at the exact spot where all the Barclay graves are situated and where we had all gathered not many weeks before. Luke Neil picked them up and cast them right the way round the churchyard and then the village, all to no avail. As in virtually every case such as this, not a hound spoke. Not even a whimper. I can see a smile on my father's face and a twinkle in his eye which would say, why didn't you cast down there?

Whilst living at Brent Pelham Hall, for as long as I could remember the foxes travelled through and around the garden at night, waking up not only the family but the hounds as well. We all knew when they had visited the churchyard, as very often they left their mark on the graves of Great Grandfather and Grandfather. However nobody can ever remember the hounds running straight to them as they did on this occasion.

Major Harold Charles Howard Taylor

1899 - 1987

It was the final day of the 1986/87 season, and our last before departing for the Fitzwilliam. My Joint Masters and I had made the decision to see if our neighbouring Masters at the Suffolk were up for a Joint Meet and sure enough they were. The venue was to be the picturesque village of Monks Eleigh which was on the border of the two Hunts. The plan was to spend half a day in each country with the more senior of the two of us, Tom Batterbee, hunting the Hounds. We had put together a pack of nine and a half couple from each pack and what a good job they made of producing such a memorable day.

My father in law Major Harold Taylor had died six weeks earlier. Born and brought up in the Badsworth country in South Yorkshire he had been a great supporter of the Essex and Suffolk for the last forty years. Unfortunately he farmed in an area which was not easily accessible during the shooting season and as a result hounds had hardly set foot on his farm for the last four seasons. This was somewhat exasperating for the Major and his daughter Lucy who I had been fortunate enough to marry the year before. However strange things were due to happen on this occasion which left us all somewhat numb and unable to explain. Was it a coincidence or something far deeper?

The land in this part of Suffolk rides very heavily and this day was no exception. It was decided to go and draw Semer Wood first, a good covert on the Essex and Suffolk side of the border which adjoined a rather intensive shoot. Luckily enough it was a place which was left totally quiet throughout the shooting season thus giving our vulpine friends a little peace from the barrage of gunfire which took place most weeks from September till the end of January.

The joint packs had settled down well whilst trotting on from the Meet and were certainly ready for action as they went in to draw the almost impenetrable bramble bushes. After a while the deep voice of Essex and Suffolk Grocer could be heard clearly as he pushed a fox up from his warm bed. It wasn't long before others joined in and the wood soon rang with their tremendous cry. After ten minutes or so, a resounding holloa came from the north eastern corner of the covert as one of those on spy duty had seen our fox stealing his way across the plough. Our pilot, believe it or not, had left pointing his mask directly for Water Mill, the home of the Major and his family. On navigating our way across the River Brett, Tom and I caught up with Hounds as they had checked in the garden. In the forty odd years of the Major living at Water Mill, hounds had never been known to run through the garden. Casting on they soon picked up his line and were away across the farm through the Chalk Pit and on the Hadleigh road, the hunt coming to an end just short of Naughton Green after a sharp 45 minutes and six miles as they ran.

During a long hack back into our draw it was decided to take Hounds and just run them through the small covert beside Bildeston Church where the Major's Funeral service had taken place just those few weeks before. This was not a place where we would normally have found because the bottom had nearly all gone but on this occasion within seconds Hounds were in and out with a brace in front of them, and they were

Overlooking the Bildeston Brook

flying. Straight over the Bildeston road and again they were heading for the Major's but this time at a pace which meant one had to really gallop to keep up with them. Firstly they swum the Bildeston Brook and then the River Brett and never looked like checking at either. We caught up with them in the farmyard having navigated some seriously difficult obstacles on the way and leaving a trail of destruction in our wake with riders experiencing serious duckings in both the River and the Bildeston Brook. Having circumnavigated the garden again this fox decided to take refuge in the Major's pit, only a hundred yards from the house. The rest of the day was spent hunting in the Suffolk country with numerous foxes on the move but there was to be no more of the excitement that we had witnessed earlier.

When visualising the day one can see those in hot pursuit floundering around in both River and Brook and, knowing the Major as I did, I feel sure he would have had a smile on his face, he so enjoyed incidents such as these!

Baron Paget of Northampton QC MFH

2nd September 1908 – 2nd January 1990

Baron Paget of Northampton QC, otherwise fondly known as 'Reggie', was born on 2nd September 1908 to a renowned Shires hunting family. He and his brother, who died young, were brought up at Sulby Hall near Welford in the heart of the Pytchley country. At that time the great Frank Freeman was hunting the hounds and his childhood would have been spent hunting with them or having odd days with the Fernie. Not only was this the golden era of foxhunting, but also being in a galloping grass country, there could not have been a better place to cut one's young teeth against those stiff Northamptonshire / Leicestershire hedges.

He was called to the Bar in 1934 and his early working life was spent practicing as a Barrister in London. He married in 1931, aged twenty three, to Miss Sybil Gibbons, who became fondly known to everybody as Nancy. During the War he served with the RNVR and then lived for sometime afterwards on the Isle of Wight where he much enjoyed sailing. Later he moved back to Leicestershire hunting mainly with the Fernie and the Quorn but also managed to fit in days with the Cottesmore and the Pytchley.

His father Guy was a man of staunch Conservative beliefs and had tried hard to ensure Reggie followed his example. However this backfired and resulted in some rather serious disagreements which led to Reggie deciding to join the Labour Party. This must have caused great alarm in certain circles, however he stuck to his principles and in the post war election of 1945 was elected as MP for Northampton. He was greatly liked by his constituents and he will long be remembered for being cheered on by the crowds of tannery workers in Northampton as the Pytchley hounds left their Boxing Day Meet. It was a solid Labour seat and he was described by one Party Official as the "Foxhunting Squire who came from a good family and had been educated at Eton."

This particular Foxhunting Squire was most proud of the fact that when he was elected to the Pytchley Mastership in 1968, it was certainly a hunt with a difference. It consisted of a Peer of the Realm - Lord Wimborne - a senior member of the Medical Profession and former Master of the Atherstone and the Westerby Bassets, Dr Eric Morrison, a businessman and farmer, James Mackaness, and himself a Labour MP and QC. This lasted for three seasons.

After serving as an MP for thirty one years he became a Life Peer in 1975. One day in the House of Lords he met a delegation of Trades Unionists whilst still dressed in his muddy hunting clothes. I am led to believe this would not have been in the slightest bit embarrassing to him as it would have been quite the most normal thing for him to do.

After a distinguished career Reggie retired and living at Lubenham near Market Harborough in the heart of the Fernie country, he continued to hunt regularly both with them and the Pytchley. This popular Labour Peer always hoped that his end would be met in a similar way to that of his Father who was killed out hunting, but that was not to be. However he would always say, in his deep gravelly voice: "All I got was a broken neck!"

Reggie Paget died on 2nd January 1990. It was his wish and very typical of this generous man that both Hunts should be given most hospitable Meets, with the port provided from the proceeds of his estate.

So, on 13th January Bruce Durno brought sixteen and a half couple of bitches to the Meet at Saddington. The breeding of the Fernie Hounds at the time mainly went back to Heythrop and Beaufort blood. However there was also an interesting touch of American in them through the Green Spring Valley which was brought in by Col Murray Smith when he left the Quorn in 1960. The day commenced with senior Master Joe Cowen giving a wonderful tribute to Reggie in front of a field of a hundred and sixty people and a very large crowd of onlookers. A minute's silence was held and just before they moved off, the car followers reported to Bruce that they had spied a fox curled up asleep in the next field. Bruce took hounds straight to the spot where they had seen him last. Not one hound spoke. He had done a total vanishing act. This was the first peculiar happening to take place that day. After achieving a twisty hunt of an hour and a half in the morning from John Ball, Furnivals and Kicklewell were then drawn blank. There was also no success in looking for outliers along the Laughton Brook, however hounds found a fox in Mr Cowens, Laughton Brake and Mrs Durno was one of those who saw him slip away. She thought there was something unusual or even strange about him. He was a very large animal with a woolly coat that almost resembled an Alsatian dog. This was something that didn't ring true to the normal Fernie fox!

Hounds came away running hard to Spring Hollow where they turned left handed and crossed the Laughton to Theddingworth road to Kicklewell. They then came back left handed along the roadside and recrossed into Laughton Brake and went down to the canal swinging left handed over the gated road back to Spring Hollow and into Bunkers Hill. Out from here they went, by the canal, over the gated road across the Lubenham road into Reggie's garden at Lubenham Lodge. Joe Cowen described this as: "Most peculiar, it was almost as though the fox were making a point of looking for Reggie". After a circuit or two around the house and garden he decided to make his course along the canal and then turned down right handed to the Lubenham / Mowsley road close to the village of Lubenham. Here he ran the old railway straight without hesitation to Reggie's Folly. This was a covert he had planted and again the fox behaved in a way that he was still trying to find him. With the Boss not at home or here at the Folly this most interesting customer decided to press on and set his mask for Gumley. Crossing the Theddingworth / Gumley road below Bunkers Hill, he went on over the canal again back through Laughton Brake, over the Mowsley road to Laughton Lodge, the Belts and Gumley Covert. Here they went out at the top end to Holloway and across the Gumley / Saddington road over Mr Rammell's holes and hounds were stopped as they ran into Gumley Wood at 4.45 pm.

This had been a top class afternoon hunt. It was almost as though this wonderful cheerful man, who was well known for having his own ideas, had orchestrated the whole thing. From the port at the Meet, to the vanishing act of the first fox, the peculiarity and size of the second, the trip round the garden and then it would seem the deliberate visit to Reggie's Folly. It was something that has left many in the Fernie country and beyond more than somewhat bemused ever since. This fox was never seen again.

Major Gerald Gundry DSO MFH

16th August 1911 – 20th Dec 1990

(The Major)

Gerald Gundry was born in Dorset on 16th August 1911. It soon became abundantly clear that this was someone with a tremendous talent. As time progressed he committed a very large part of his life not only to hunting but to all those who make our sport possible, and whatever background they came from was of no consequence to him. Little did anybody know at the time, although one may have had a good guess, but Gerald Gundry was to become one of the best loved characters that foxhunting in this country has ever produced. The Major, as he became fondly known, is still spoken about with great affection not only in the country hunted by the Duke of Beaufort's Hounds but in far wider circles, and this is some twenty four years after his death. He became a legend and that was purely and simply down to the standards he set himself in always putting others first.

Gerald's father owned and ran Gundry's Rope and Netmakers in Bridport, Dorset. This company had been set up by a Joseph Gundry in 1665 and was still operating under its own name until 1963. Gerald was brought up by his grandfather, Parson Milne, who was at the time Master of the Cattistock, a position he held for thirty one seasons. It was during his early life that Gerald developed a deep faith, and this, combined with a strong commitment to hunting, is more than likely why he made such a first class Master of Foxhounds.

He joined the 16th/5th Lancers and during the War went out to serve in Italy where he was injured. After recovering he was posted to India and whilst he was out there the news came through to the now Major Gundry, that His Grace the Duke of Beaufort (otherwise known as Master by his many friends) was looking for a Hunt Secretary. A telegram was quickly sent to Badminton applying for the position. Unfortunately the telegram was signed off as being from Ghandi, not Gundry. "That is the last sort of person I want," Master is reputed to have said. Any misunderstandings were quickly cleared up and the Major was swiftly appointed. However in 1951 Master decided he wanted him as his Joint Master, which seemed a natural progression, and it was here he was to remain until 1985. What the Major put into running this very large Hunt, was immeasurable. He was the eyes and ears that every hunting country needs to make it tick. Most importantly he had the knowledge in knowing when to act swiftly which, still today, is of the utmost importance. I well remember him telling me that on taking up his position on 1st May he did not have long to learn the country,

The Duke of Beaufort's Hounds returning home from exercise

as that year they started hunting on the 26TH July and finished up in Lower Woods on the 15ᵗʰ May. He was someone though who relished the challenge that the Duke of Beaufort and his hounds could bring.

For twenty-four years the Major shared the hunting of the hounds, initially with Master and occasionally Bert Pateman and latterly with the late Brian Gupwell. He hunted either the doghounds or a mixed pack and the sport they showed was outstanding. He knew exactly what to do to entertain the large Beaufort Fields who would be out on the days he was to perform. He was someone who would not tolerate any nonsense but at the same time would always have a twinkle in his eye which often eased the situation. On one occasion he nearly met his Maker rather sooner than he anticipated. Whilst blowing hard for his hounds, he burst a duodenal ulcer. The Major was rushed off to Swindon Hospital with only a fifty / fifty chance of survival. The poor old hounds were in some sort of disarray and were taken back to the lorry and loaded up to go back to Badminton. However suddenly they burst into song and there they sat singing for a considerable while. They were obviously missing the boss but what a tribute to him. However it was not long before he was back in action and normal business resumed.

For those of us who were fortunate enough to have witnessed the Major hunting hounds, it was quite an experience as you always knew something was going to happen which would stir the blood. His fox sense and tenacity made the whole operation run like clockwork with many long hunts achieved over large parts of the Beaufort country. An absolute all-rounder could not be a better description of the man, and his management of the Beaufort country was something that had to be admired. Not only did he make it his business to know each landowner or farmer, everybody, and I mean everybody, mattered and quite rightly so, whatever their age or whoever they were. Travelling round the Beaufort country, the old pale green Land Rover would often come to a halt if he saw someone who he felt just needed a kindly word. More often than not something important would be learnt from the conversation such as where the nearest litter of cubs had been born or, on the last day's hunting in the area, where the hunted fox had disappeared to. He was certainly a one off, but the respect he was held in said it all. The Major knew absolutely everything that was going on around him.

Retiring from the Mastership with a bad back did not come easy. In fact, after the presentation ceremony had taken place at Badminton in April 1978, Master announced: "The Major is going to continue!" Sure enough he did until 1985 and with just as much enthusiasm as before. His Grace sadly died on 5ᵗʰ February 1985 and Captain Ian Farquhar was appointed by the Eleventh Duke as his Joint Master. The Captain took on the hunting of hounds and in his own distinctive style made a very good job of it. The Major watched and observed the new regime's every move with, we have to say, a certain amount of scrutiny. Over the ensuing years age started to weary him and he died on Thursday 20ᵗʰ December 1990. However, never one to stop from inspiring others, in the last few months of his life he came up with the brilliant idea that a new educational audio tape should be made to teach and encourage those fresh to hunting about the calls on the hunting horn. Sadly he died shortly before it came to fruition, and it is now in the hands of many hunting enthusiasts both here and abroad. Quite rightly it is dedicated to him and when we listen carefully we can hear hounds running, then his wonderful gravelly voice explaining where the fox has gone and lastly what the Huntsman is blowing. We know then what a real depth of knowledge there was and just how much those of us who have come after have benefited from all he taught us.

The Major always said that should he die in the season the hounds must not stop hunting and this wish was very much adhered to by the Eleventh Duke and the Captain. Two days later, on Saturday 22ⁿᵈ December, they met at Easton Grey, a small village close to the Major's home at Shipton Moyne. Foxes are always plentiful in this part of the Beaufort country, with such coverts as Silk Wood, Garden Plantation always being a sure find. However something was amiss this day. Every covert, every hedgerow, every rough corner was blank. Not a sniff anywhere. This was unusual, but as in all hunting countries our quarry is very good at making fools of us, so one could say it is not totally extraordinary. That said at this particular time, it did seem a bit odd.

After Second Horses more country was drawn, all to no avail, when suddenly hounds marked at what is described in Gloucestershire as a gateway drot, at the back of Tugwell's Gorse. For those who have not heard of one of these before, a drot is a short pipe under a field gateway. As you can imagine, with the fox hearing hounds at one end, he was soon gone. For the next forty minutes they hunted beautifully down to Easton Grey over the road through Wetlands and out to Pond Farm. They then turned up towards Estcourt before swinging left handed to Tanners Covert. The Captain was coming up the Westonbirt / Shipton Moyne road when he got a view of the fox crossing and going into the garden of Clayfields, where the Major and his family had lived for many years. When he got there hounds were casting round on the gravel in front of the house. The foot followers had seen him go in but not out, but his hunch told him that the fox must have gone straight through and as a result began to make his move. Suddenly two hounds shot into a bush right beside the front door, out came the fox and it was there they caught him, on the doorstep. There was a stunned silence and the spines of all those who were still in attendance shivered but just a little later more was to come. The Captain collected his hounds together and went on and drew again. They did not find. Whilst they were hacking homewards back past Clayfields, Jane, the Major's daughter, came out and asked the Captain: "Ian, what time did you catch that fox?" He looked at his watch and said with meticulous accuracy, "Jane, it was twenty eight minutes to four." There was a stunned silence. It was the exact time to the minute, forty eight hours before, that the Major had passed away.

On Christmas Eve 1990, the Major was taken on his final journey. It was not long after they left home, both Robin and Jane happened to realise they were following the Beaufort Hounds who, at that very same time were on the way to the Meet. As we can imagine no one would have been more pleased about this than the Major.

Is anybody I wonder ever going to be able to explain the occurrences that took place over those few days? I don't think so, but mark my word it all turned out just as the Major would have wanted, except possibly the shortage of foxes on the day from Easton Grey!

Jeff Davey
1941 - 1994
Head Keeper to the Walcot Estate

Jeff Davey could best be described as a gentle giant. He originally came to farm at Mill Farm, Barnack near Stamford before becoming Head Keeper to the Dennis family who own and farm a large acreage of Lincolnshire and Cambridgeshire. Walcot Hall is in the Fitzwilliam country and is situated between the Burghley and Milton Estates. It is also near to the picturesque village of Barnack, famous for its stone which was shipped down the Rivers Nene and Ouse to build Peterborough and Ely Cathedrals.

The main interest on the Estate is shooting but a healthy relationship has existed between that and hunting here, the two sports having for many years run alongside each other, with the hounds being allowed access during the early part of the season and then again in February. However in this particular year of 1994 both the owner Darby Dennis and Jeff Davey had agreed for the hounds to draw the home coverts in November.

In this summer my wife Lucy and I and our two boys, Ben and Rowley, came from Milton Park to live in the neighbouring village of Southorpe. In the middle of our very first night we were awoken by, believe it or not, foxes fighting on the front doorstep. This was something of a surprise to say the least, despite the fact we knew it was a reasonably well foxed area. Even more of a shock to the system was when Jeff called round at breakfast time the following morning to ask if I had brought some foxes with me. Three had shot out of our drive right in front of him, whilst he was out on night watch.

A couple of months later, Jeff died very suddenly while working in the Estate woodyard. This was a tremendous shock to everybody who knew and worked with him. He was a most kind and generous man who was very well liked and respected in the local area. As much as anything he would also be remembered for the odd practical joke that he would play on some poor unsuspecting local, the MFH being one who he caught out on more than one occasion.

After Jeff's tragic death, discussions took place as to whether we should continue to hunt the Estate as planned for the second Saturday in November. It was decided to go ahead and that the hounds would meet in Southorpe. As it turned out the village people most generously clubbed together and we were lavishly entertained. A great crowd of all ages attended. There was absolutely no doubt that Jeff was very much on our minds on that day and even more so after the extraordinary happenings that were to take place within an hour of the hounds moving off.

Walcot Big Wood was looking its best and there was a real autumnal feel to the day as George Adams put the Fitzwilliam mixed pack in to draw. Normally there would be a large herd of fallow deer in residence but today for some unknown reason they were absent. When the hounds got themselves into the box bushes on the Primrose Walk, they soon found a big old fox, who gave the appearance of having been around for a year or two. This was Jeff's favourite part of Big Wood and was where he would come and sit to observe the natural world around him. It was also the exact spot where only a month before his ashes had been laid to rest. They hunted slowly at first but as time went on, the momentum picked up and they really began to gather up some speed. After a circuit of Big Wood hounds were now heading fast down towards the Hall, so kicking on I decided to go and stand quietly outside the front door and watch the large area of lawn and gravel. Suddenly

The Gardens at Walcot Hall

I saw him coming towards me. Hounds were beginning to fly but not this fellar. He knew exactly what he was doing and where he was going. He trotted on until he was quite close and then he stopped dead in his tracks and stared straight at me. I could not quite believe what I was seeing.

A minute is a very long time in a situation like this and it wasn't until the lead hounds appeared on the lawn that he lolloped off at his own pace down the front drive. He then jumped up onto the wall which surrounded the woodyard and ran exactly across to where Jeff had died. Here he hesitated for a second or two as the hounds couldn't quite jump the wall. Then he came out on the back drive along which he ran for fifty yards towards the Southorpe road before turning right handed and disappearing under Jeff's garden gate. Hounds hunted up to that exact spot and that, as they say, was that. It was yet another example of our quarry deciding to disappear into thin air. George Adams cast his hounds right the way round, all to no avail.

I have often looked back on this particular day and the only thought I could come up with was, that old fox was sent by Jeff to remind me just how lucky we were to have been allowed to hunt the Walcot Estate in the middle of the shooting season. If not it was Jeff himself having the last laugh on all of us, who not only knew him but had great respect for this wonderful countryman who had now gone on to the other place. We will never know.

The Hon Lady Elizabeth Ann Hastings DL MFH
1934 -1997

Born in 1934 The Hon Lady Hastings (or Lizzie Anne) was one of the most popular and admired people I have been privileged to meet. The kindness and support she gave to people from all different walks of life will be remembered for very many years. She showed a great sense of care to all her staff at Milton as well as the other family estates, at Wentworth, Malton and Strines. The loyalty and high esteem in which she was held was plain to see.

Lizzie Anne was a devout Roman Catholic who came to live at Milton soon after Lord Fitzwilliam's death in 1980. With her husband Sir Stephen Hastings, previously Conservative MP for mid Bedfordshire, she took on the Mastership of the family pack. Although Lizzie Anne never hunted on a horse the Fitzwilliam Hounds were an integral part of the Estate and the surrounding area. Lizzie Anne never forgot the responsibilities that went with that position, particularly to the farmers and their families up and down the country. She had a particular fascination for the breeding of the Fitzwilliam Hounds and with sound advice from the late Duke of Beaufort and Sir Peter Farquhar she bred a pack ideally suited to the Cambridgeshire and Northamptonshire ploughs. Indeed I was more than honoured when Lizzie Anne handed on this responsibility to me in the early '90s.

Milton Hall which was a magnet to the local fox population

During the next ten years we all gained a huge amount of pleasure from our Mastership, then suddenly in the early summer of 1996 Lizzie Anne told me the devastating news that she had been diagnosed with the dreaded cancer. Despite putting up one hell of a fight, it beat her in March 1997. We had all lost someone whom we adored. Not long before she died she asked if I would go and see her early one evening. As always she was interested in the hounds and we talked about everything from how they had been hunting to what we were breeding from. Two hours flew by but fascinatingly one of Lizzie Anne's main concerns was that we did not draw the West End, a good covert which is nearest the house, for the remainder of the season. There was no other reason for it except that she felt the vixen who we all knew for being a bit smaller than most was due to have cubs somewhere nearby, and she felt the old girl ought to be left quietly to get on with what all good vixens do in March and April.

Lizzie Anne died peacefully on Thursday 16th March 1997 and people from every walk of life turned up for her funeral a few days later. After everyone had departed for home, Sir Stephen asked me to go up and have a drink with him. This I duly did and as I drove up to the West End of the house with the stable clock striking seven, there was our mutual friend sitting on the doorstep. As I picked her up in the car lights she slowly slipped off through the iron railings across the corner of the park and back into the covert. On mentioning this to Reverend William Burke, who earlier that day had taken the funeral service, he told me with absolute confidence: "That is, James, a sure sign that all is well."

Nobody would have been more pleased than Lizzie Anne, when on the first morning the following season, from the meet at kennels, West End was as always drawn and held a very strong and healthy litter of cubs.

Sure enough Lizzie Anne had been right and the Vicar's words rang true. All was well and our greatest friend was now at peace.

* * * * *

The behaviour of our Milton vixen on the evening of Lady Hastings' Funeral was extraordinary to say the least. What perhaps is even more peculiar was for there to be another incident on the family's Wentworth Estate, just a few days later. Wentworth was historically the most senior of the Fitzwilliam Estates and is situated in the heartland of industrial South Yorkshire, no more than five miles from the outskirts of Sheffield, Rotherham and Barnsley. It was an area that was famous for and proud of its coal mining tradition and to this day you can still clearly see the remains of long gone collieries reminding us of a very important past.

Wentworth Woodhouse played an important part of hunting's history in South Yorkshire

It was of course coal which not only brought the Fitzwilliams their wealth but with it came the huge respect the miners had for their employers. It is a fact that those working for the Fitzwilliams became the envy of the miners working in other private pits in the area. In 1926 at the time of the National Strike, Lord 'Billy' Fitzwilliam not only instructed his men to strike but to bring the pit ponies up to the front of the house for them, where they were to be taught how to play polo. During this time the Fitzwilliam (Wentworth) Hounds were kennelled in the village and hunted the surrounding area. It was indeed a private pack, however it was also a Hunt that received considerable support from those who, when not working below ground, enjoyed the pleasures the chase could bring them.

During the early '90s we brought the Fitzwilliam (Milton) Hounds up to mark the 60th anniversary of the disbandment of the Fitzwilliam (Wentworth) Hounds. Among the huge crowd that attended the Meet in front of Wentworth Woodhouse that day were Sir Stephen and the Hon. Lady Hastings and many retired miners and their families who either walked, drove or came on the bus from nearby former colliery villages such as Elsecar, especially for the occasion. Their memories were a pleasure to listen to and the real South Yorkshire welcome they gave Lady Hastings was something that was a joy to see and it will last long with all of us, who indeed were privileged to be there.

After the Wentworth Hounds had been dispersed, the Kennels were converted into a fine dwelling that linked up to the Huntsman's House and this is where Sir Stephen and Lady Hastings would reside when on Wentworth business. There was no doubt it was an unusual feeling, when staying there, as the bedroom I used just happened to be a beautifully converted hound lodge with pictures of the Wentworth Hounds adorning the walls.

If I have digressed I apologise, but feel in this case it is important to build up a picture of the importance of Wentworth in relation to the true and most moving occurrence that took place that day.

David Randall was hunting the Badsworth at the time as they had incorporated Wentworth into their country before handing it over latterly to the Grove and Rufford, on their amalgamation with the Bramham Moor. On this occasion the Hounds had met at John Ambler's house (the Head Keeper) in the park. It was mid March 1997, just ten days at the very most after Lady Hastings' death. David knew the country well and related to me in detail exactly what happened that day. This is where the link between a Huntsman and his Hounds becomes clear, as the country is far from easy and the trust of which we speak becomes of key importance. The outlying coverts were blank, however on going to the Trowes, a low lying thick place just off the Sheffield road, they found. For the next two hours they pulled off something that can only be described as a good old fashioned hound hunt, which demonstrated some of the very finest examples of venery to be found in the 20th century.

The fox started by taking a course which took hounds within half a field of the housing estates of Scholes before turning away left handed into Rockingham Wood. After hunting round here for a while they came away down to the lakes and then on into Morley Wood before crossing the big open fields into the Mausoleum and on to the Fox Covert. From here he made his way up to the main Rotherham road where the car followers swore blind that he had not crossed. Much time was lost as David then cast back through the covert to no avail. Hunches are very important to a Huntsman and they can be invaluable in difficult situations, especially when you could be in danger of losing your quarry. He took them over the road and cast them up the ditch towards Hoober Plantation and Hoober Stand and away they went as hard as they could go until they hit some ground which had been newly spread with muck and this was when true fox sense again had to be brought to the fore to see what he had done next. However touching a line into Giles Plantation it was just looking as though the end of the hunt had come, as scent had virtually given out, when one of the Under Keepers saw the hunted fox cross the road into Needles Eye.

This changed things and they really began to fly. Running on into Kings Wood, they took a line down to the now derelict site of Elsecar Colliery, ran through the remaining outbuildings and on as hard as they could go to the back of Wentworth village and to the Woodyard. It was thought that the fox had crossed the main road into the Deer Park, but he had been headed and Saintly was the only one who could hunt his line back into the field adjoining the old Kennels where they checked. Here David observed some of his older hounds were showing interest at a gate into Sir Stephen and Lady Hastings' garden. A key was found and an exhaustive search began. After a while it looked as though it was fruitless, when suddenly the hounds lifted their heads and raced towards a large patch of rhododendrons. Out shot the fox and his end came in a matter of seconds, right on the front doorstep of what had been home to the last Huntsman of the Fitzwilliam (Wentworth) Foxhounds and up until just a few days before, the South Yorkshire residence of the Lady Master of the Fitzwilliam (Milton) Foxhounds!

* * * * *

A number of years after Lady Hastings' death I was fortunate enough to witness another most unusual occurrence. It was on the day of the Opening Meet and a very large crowd of people were out both on horses and in cars. Hounds had been busy in and around the Park at Milton all morning and it was when they went into the large covert, Thistlemoor, that they really started to go up a gear. Hunting with a lovely cry, the fox came away towards the house but was headed by the cars. With that he turned back to where he had been

found with the pack gaining on him all the time. It would seem that the end result was becoming increasingly inevitable, however he reached the post and rails just in time, slipped through the wire netting and, you would have thought, disappeared. Not a bit of it. For a few seconds he stood there on the other side and stared straight at his pursuers. Then off he went, in his own time.

George Adams bringing the Fitzwilliam Hounds back from the Family Graves

A few minutes later he was hollered away at the north western corner of the covert and was viewed making his way towards Marholm village. Crossing the Castor road, he went through the hedge and was seen going in the direction of Marholm Church. For a moment he disappeared into a garden where somebody was burning some leaves, but out he came and ran up beside the churchyard right into the corner where Lady Hastings, Sir Stephen, and Lord and Lady Fitzwilliam are all buried. Turning back on himself he retraced his steps almost exactly the way he came and was last seen leaving Thistlemoor to go back towards the Hall.

Hounds however ran to the corner by the graves and could not take his line a yard further. Whether this was the smoke from the fire which had drifted that far, although I very much doubt that, or was it yet another one of those strange coincidences? There were several different aspects that came out of this hunt which I was most fortunate to witness and found most intriguing. They were, firstly seeing the fox coming back across Milton Park with the hounds in close contention, the next was of him standing and staring straight at his pursuers, and then witnessing them hunting down beside Marholm Churchyard. However, when George Adams stopped, blew for the hounds and took them back, there right in front of me was a beam of sunlight shining down upon the family graves where the hounds had been a few seconds before. It was then that I really felt a chill go down my spine.

Not only was I lucky enough to witness this first hand, I just happened to have a camera with me at each stage of the hunt.

Frank Dallyn

1923 -1999

Harbourer to the Devon and Somerset Staghounds

It is now the turn of the wild Red Deer of Exmoor to play their part in a moving and unusual experience which took place shortly after the death of the very well respected Harbourer to the Devon and Somerset Staghounds, Frank Dallyn.

First and most important I think it would be wise to furnish you with some information about Frank. This will hopefully help give an insight into this fascinating character. I have to thank Anne Chown, Frank's partner, for supplying me with the relevant details about what happened on this special day.

Frank Smyth Dallyn was born on 26th April 1923 at Challacombe Mill during the last few days of the spring staghunting season. He was born into a life which was steeped in farming and hunting. What more could a man wish for? The skills he learnt from his father both in agriculture and horsemanship were immense. Moving from Challacombe to Bratton Fleming when he was ten, their time was spent milking cows and breaking in young horses. He and his father would go out to a farm on the Moor and drive a colt back to Hunnacott without a halter, just loose. This is something that you certainly would not see today.

Frank then moved to Simonsbath where he continued to break in young horses. The next year he was asked to be Stud Groom at the Devon and Somerset kennels for the season and the following to whip in. During Norah Harding's Mastership Frank was asked if he would take on the role of Harbourer in the northern part of the Devon and Somerset country. He was delighted to accept this challenge and felt very privileged to be given this opportunity. As you can imagine, being a man with his upbringing, he was to carry out his task to perfection.

Red deer during the summer months

Harbouring the deer for a day's hunting is a real craft, the detail of which would make a fascinating book in its own right. However to go out at dusk and watch or track them (or slotting as it is often called) and then to be out at first light to locate the animal which is to be hunted, is a skill only known to a very few. The most important ingredient must be to have a high level of patience and to develop a deep understanding of the countryside and what is happening around you day by day. Learning the habits of the wild red deer only comes to you after many years of quiet and careful observation. This was something that came to Frank Dallyn entirely naturally.

For the next nine years Frank would have been out in all types of weather until sadly ill health forced him to retire from this most valuable post. On his last day he harboured seven stags on the Deer Park above Simonsbath. He went to the Meet like all good Harbourers and reported to the Huntsman, the late Dennis Boyles, what he had seen and gave him the recent whereabouts of the deer, he then went home. Anne knew he was very ill, however after a series of operations he managed to go hunting in the car and was kept up to date with what was going on at regular intervals. He was keen to know about his beloved deer and where they had run to. Woe betide the messenger if they got it wrong.

During the last few months Frank was in and out of hospital and nursing homes until the time he came home to Exmoor, the place he loved best. The tragic death of his son Dennis seemed too hard a blow for Frank to cope with and he died peacefully at home on 8th October 1999.

At the end of autumn Staghunting Anne decided to go quietly on her own to take Frank's ashes down to Buscombe Beeches. This is a place which takes its name from where years before a bank of beech trees had been carefully planted into which sheep could be herded. This was long before the advent of wire netting. It was also where Frank spent many happy times over the years schooling various different horses. That day the Devon and Somerset met at Brendon Two Gates but no one had a clue that Anne was going to be anywhere in the vicinity. She lived in hope that something might materialise but what was to happen was to exceed every expectation she could ever have dreamt. This is one of the wildest parts of Exmoor and as Anne walked in from the road with her head bowed against a very strong wind she had no idea what was happening behind her. Suddenly Anne realised she was being followed by the whole Field, which had appeared as if from nowhere. She trudged on down into Buscombe Combe where Frank's ashes were to be scattered. The hounds were by now a considerable distance away and she had every reason to believe the Field were long gone out across the forest. What was to happen next was not only to astound Anne but also all of those who have been honoured to hear her experiences.

Anne had just finished laying Frank's ashes in amongst the trees at Buscombe Beeches when all of a sudden she noticed no more than thirty yards away from her were two stags, one with five hinds, coming down each side of the combe. They slowly crossed the water and it was at that point the most peculiar thing happened. The deer stopped right opposite Anne and looked straight in her direction. They were at total ease and in no hurry whatsoever. After a little while they trotted on making their way down towards Hoccombe Water. Some moments later she thought she could hear hounds running and it wasn't long before the cry of the Devon and Somerset Staghounds became evident. Then suddenly, with five and a half couple of tufters on his heels, there was the hunted stag right in front of her. This time however he was going at a somewhat swifter speed than his colleagues had been a little earlier.

Anne climbed back to the top of the hill and there was the entire Devon and Somerset field waiting in the same place as she had left them earlier that morning.

On this extraordinary day it really seemed that the Red deer of Exmoor, the Devon and Somerset Staghounds as well as their Masters, Subscribers, Supporters and Staff all came together in a totally uncanny way to say "Goodbye" to their great friend and colleague, Frank Dallyn. If anybody had tried to plan this, it would never have worked. It was just meant to be.

To my mind the Staghunting Song of Exmoor would appear to be one of the finest tributes to Frank, so here it is below:

The Staghunting Song of Exmoor

The Forest above and the combe below
On a bright September morn
He's the Soul of Clod who thanks not God
That ever his body was born.
So hurry along the Stag's afoot
The Master's up and away!
Halloo! Halloo!!
We'll follow it through
From Bratton to Porlock Bay

Chorus

So hurry along the Stag's afoot
The Master's up and away!
Halloo! Halloo! We'll follow it through
From Bratton to Porlock Bay!

Hark to the Tufters challenge true
T'is a note the Red Deer knows,
His courage awakes; his covert he breaks,
And up for the Moor he goes!
He's all his rights and seven on top,
His eyes o'a King
And he'll beggar the pride of some that ride
Before he leaves the ling!

Chorus

Here comes the Huntsman bringing the pack,
Steady! He's laying them on!
By the sound of their chime you may tell it's time
To harden your hearts and be gone
Nightacott, Narracott and Hunnacott's* passed
Right for the North they face
He's leading them straight for Blackmoor Gate,
And he's setting a pounding pace

*Hunnacott is where Frank Dallyn farmed

Chorus

We're running him now on a breast high scent
But he leaves us standing still,
When we swing round by Wistland Pound
He's far up Challacombe Hill.
The pack is a string of struggling hounds
The quarry's a dancing midge,
They're trying their reins on the edge of the chains
Whilst he's on Cheriton Ridge

Chorus

He's gone by Kittuck and Lucott Moor,
He's gone by Woodcock's Ley,
By the little white town he's turned him down
And he's running by open sea
So hurry along we'll both be in,
The crowd's a parish away!
We're a field or two and we've followed it through
From Bratton to Porlock Bay

Chorus

So hurry along we'll both be in,
The crowd are a parish away!
We're a field a two and we've followed it through
From Bratton to Porlock Bay

Looking across the Burghley Lake to the gardens where the Marquis of Exeter is buried

The Marquis of Exeter KCMG MFH

1905 – 1981

During the 1970s and '80s it was customary for the Fitzwilliam hounds to meet at the old Burghley Kennels on the Saturday after the Horse Trials. There could not have been a more beautiful place to go hunting at the start of autumn. To observe the mist rising from the lake in the early hours of the morning with the house appearing to be like a ship out at sea was an experience never to be forgotten.

The late Marquis of Exeter had been an extremely popular man. Although I sadly never met him, it is well recorded that his enthusiasm for whatever he did in life was infectious. He became a World class athlete winning the gold medal for the 440 yards hurdle race at the 1928 Amsterdam Olympics. His hunting career was equally distinguished having been Master and Huntsman of the East Sussex and the Old Berks before returning back to his family home at Burghley in 1958 to re-form the family pack which had first been disbanded in 1938. The country he hunted was loaned to him by the Cottesmore, Fitzwilliam and the Belvoir and there was hardly a piece of land which was out of bounds. The farmers who hunted with him held him in extremely high esteem.

His Lordship's enthusiasm for the chase started at the age of nine when, like his Grace the tenth Duke of Beaufort, he started hunting his own private pack of Harriers. This was to give the pair of them the thorough grounding they required to hunt a pack of hounds successfully. With Sid Pepper, the Head Keeper at his side, the foundation stones of a lifetime interest in hunting were soon being laid. It would appear that the Marquis' popularity with every different section of society would, one could imagine, also very soon and most fittingly spread to his hounds. Bill Garrett, who later became his First Whip and Kennel Huntsman at the Old Berks and then the Burghley, would bring the hounds on to the Meets and wait for the Marquis to arrive. On hearing his vehicle and without them actually being able see him they would suddenly put their heads in the air and start to sing. Maybe they had learnt this from their Master who it was said had a most melodious voice. Sadly at the end of the 1968 / '69 season the Burghley Hounds were disbanded.

It was a Saturday morning in the September of 1989, just twenty years after the Burghley had ceased to exist, when we were to meet with the Fitzwilliam Hounds at their old Kennels. The Park which was so carefully

Photograph by Jim Meads

The Marquis of Exeter with his Burghley Hounds in 1967

created by Capability Brown looked at its best. The sun rising across it from the east and with the Canada Geese already in full cry, there was no more perfect morning imaginable.

Immediately behind the kennels lay the gardens and this was our first draw. Although part of the gardens were ornamental, at that time the rest was a mass of brambles and snowberry bushes, an ideal spot to find a litter of cubs. The covert ran alongside the lake and approximately half way round and about fifty yards up into the covert is where the Marquis had been laid to rest some eight years before. His grave is reached by a narrow path that runs down from the southern side of the Park and is where I would often go and quietly watch the action.

It was not too long on this occasion before a hound spoke and then another and shortly afterwards the deep cry of the Fitzwilliam hounds was soon resounding around the covert and echoing off the lake. For the next two hours they hunted beautifully in and around the Gardens, Big Holt and the Butlands where eventually they worked their way up to a fox at the very top end.

The covert is a good mile and a half long but at the most a hundred yards wide. In places it was very thick and in other parts hounds were really able to make the best of it. They were beginning to motor on and as I was not hunting hounds at the time, I was able to push ahead and could see the fox at regular intervals. He was twisting and turning, managing to keep a reasonable distance between him and his pursuers. However as they crossed back into the gardens the gap had narrowed significantly and it looked as though it would all be over in a matter of seconds. I quickly made my way to the graveside and within no time he was there. He jumped up on the stone wall and ran across His Lordship's Grave with Fitzwilliam Gavin just about to catch him. The rest of the pack were there too. Gavin and the fox jumped off the wall on the other side almost together, but instead of seeing what I was expecting, there was this third season Fitzwilliam dog hound with his head up and no sign whatsoever of his quarry. Not a hound spoke again. Our fox quite literally had, it would seem like others, disappeared into thin air!

Not long after this Lady Victoria Leatham, Lord Exeter's daughter, kindly gave me his hunting horn. It is something that will always be treasured and be a reminder of this quite extraordinary experience.

Willie Porter MFH *1879 -1952*
Jack Porter MFH *1912 -1991*

It is family links with various packs of hounds which go back over a century that make hunting history so fascinating. The Porters from the Eskdale and Ennerdale have more than demonstrated their true commitment in keeping hunting going in what is still in one of the wildest parts of England. In 1857 Thomas Dobson became Master and remained in charge until 1910 when he handed over to William Porter who had been hunting the hounds for him for some considerable years. William's son Jack then took the hounds on in 1953.

Whilst out hunting at Wasdale his father collapsed and died. A memorial stone still stands at the exact spot where this great Fell Huntsman passed away. Edmund joined his father Jack in 1978 and hunted hounds until 2008. He was rated by the legendary Captain Wallace as one of the best Huntsmen that he had ever seen. In fact it was the Eskdale and Ennerdale that the Captain also turned to for the first fell outcross on his Heythrop bitches. That is something for Edmund and all who hunted with him to be extremely proud of. It is nice to hear the Porter's sons, Andrew and David, are as keen as their forebears. This certainly bodes well for the future of the Eskdale and Ennerdale Hunt.

Watching and waiting

When Thursday 17th February 2005 came every single one of us with hunting in our veins came close to tears as the iniquitous legislation that we had tried so hard to fight off finally became reality. In every part of England there was a deep sense of sadness that hung over the countryside like a dark cloud. Nobody knew what the future would hold. However it was not long before we regained our strength, pulled ourselves together and started to make those who had initiated such bad law look like the fools they were. Come what may and in whatever form it was to take, the fight back soon began. So when the Eskdale and Ennerdale Hounds met at their kennels at Sword House for what appeared to be the last time, it was most understandably a very emotional day for everybody concerned.

The strange incidents that have been recorded in this book all have their own individual charm. This one though will always stand out for two reasons, first because of the date it took place and the desperate situation hunting found itself in and second, why should a hunted fox do what it decided to do on that day and not on one of the many other occasions over the years that the hounds had hunted in the area of the Southern Lakes?

After a most hospitable meet, Edmund moved off with sixteen couple of pure Fell Hounds and loosed them off into the bracken bed behind the Kennels where they found quickly. Hounds hunted round the Rigg before crossing the road onto Field Head Fell. Luckily the fox was turned away from the most dangerous spot of Dry Ghyll and was also kept out of the Borran before he ran up the valley past Stanley Ghyll Waterfalls. Here they dropped in to cross the River Esk and ran out onto Hodge Howe. Coming back in they were flying by now and went on past St Catherine's Church in Boot, where they narrowly missed Tommy Dobson's grave. This incidentally is where Willie Porter, Jack Porter and Arthur Irving are all laid to rest and up to 2005 they were the only other men to have hunted the Eskdale and Ennerdale Hounds. Re-crossing the Esk they made their way back to the Rigg in quick time before attempting to go back to Dry Ghyll. Turning away again the fox went down the valley to Field Head Farm where they caught him in the field next to the yard. This had been a first class hunt of just on two hours with the fox not only running past the graves of four out of the five great Fellmen, but they caught the fox beside the farmyard where both Willie and Jack Porter had farmed for many years.

In the history of the Eskdale and Ennerdale Hunt nothing like this had ever occurred before.

Violet Mary Wright

18th December 1935 – 3rd April 2004

I have written a piece here in dedication to a wonderful person, Violet Mary Wright. Although her husband Ray hunted with the Cottesmore in the car, Mary didn't. The peculiar happening which took place on this beautiful spring day however had no relevance whatsoever to hunting. Believe it or not it is a herd of Friesian dairy cows in the small farming village of Freeby in Leicestershire that find themselves in the limelight on this occasion. There are those hardened cynics who may say that what you are about to read is purely and simply a coincidence and nothing else. However all the instances you read here are true and have been witnessed by many different people from up and down the country as well as abroad. Those of us who were present were incredibly moved that anything like it should actually take place before our very eyes.

Violet Mary Wright, or Mary to all who knew her well, was born in Melton Mowbray on 18th December 1935. Her father was a groom at a time when Melton had the reputation of being the capital of English foxhunting. It was of course the place where Royalty would come and spend many happy hours in the saddle either hunting with the Belvoir, Quorn or Cottesmore. Then as many as two hundred second horsemen would be seen hacking out of the town to a central point where they would meet the hounds from whichever pack they were sent to. Whilst Melton is known today as being hunting's original centre, at that time there was no doubt it was a real hub of activity both by day and also more than likely by night.

Mary's childhood was spent living in Melton and was where she went to school before progressing to find employment as a telephonist at a shoe factory in the town. She then moved on to working as an operator at the GPO who ran the telephone exchange. Ray and Mary married on 21st August 1954 with Mary continuing to work on the exchange and Ray as a general farm worker for Jack Darke at Freeby. Mary was very keen at the time on sport and played a lot of Badminton, which she was very good at, and was well recognised as one of the top players in the area.

After a while Lord Gretton offered Ray the position as Cowman to his Whissendine herd of 150 Friesians. This he duly took and it wasn't long before he was well into his stride. Being such an extremely hard worker, life with Mary at his side was made somewhat easier. Having given up her work for the GPO it was her job to feed sixty calves and rear them from four days old till three months with all the heifers going in as replacements to the dairy herd. However Mary had Ray exactly where she wanted him and stood no nonsense whatsoever, which was just as well as her responsibilities also took in the cleaning of the milking parlour.

Mary was someone who always liked to have plenty to do and during the summer when there were no calves to look after she returned to Melton to work on the switchboard until 1990 when they both retired. Her next challenge was looking after her elderly mother before becoming a carer at the Barleythorpe Old People's

Home near Oakham. While Mary was working here she suddenly became seriously ill and tragically died two months later. The local area, and most of all Ray, had lost somebody very special and as you will have gathered a person who was never shy of hard graft.

Mary was buried at Freeby in Leicestershire on a beautiful early April day. As the large congregation gathered at the graveside to pay their last respects, a most moving experience was about to take place right in front of us. As Mary was about to complete her final journey we looked up to see a procession of dry cows walking down the adjoining field towards us and it would seem they had a sense of purpose on this day, which was highly unusual. Cattle, you would have thought, would not normally like to find themselves too close to large crowds of people but this lot were totally unfazed and kept on coming in our direction until they reached the churchyard fence. This was no more than eight to ten yards from where we were all standing. They then spread out and bowed their heads for some few minutes. Then, they lifted their heads up and proceeded to walk back into the middle of the field where they stood back and watched us. It was exactly as though they had come down the field deliberately to pay their last respects to Mary. I have never witnessed anything quite like it before nor had any of those who were there that day. It made what was a very sad day one to remember for the most moving of reasons and I can imagine Mary loving it.

Winifred Mooris

12th February 1907 - 25th March 1999

Kind and generous are without doubt just two of the most apt words which would describe this remarkable lady who hunted with the Iroquois Hunt in the United States for very many years. She was one of the truest friends to hunting anyone could have ever wished to meet and was held in very high esteem by all who knew her. Although sadly I never had the honour of meeting Winifred, I am indebted to Jerry Miller, Master of the Iroqouis, and their Huntsman Lilla Mason for furnishing me with some most fascinating details about this remarkable person.

Winifred Mooris decided to purchase some land from the proceeds of the sale of her famous stallion Munchenhaussen. She donated a small piece for the Episcopal Church of St. Hubert to be built, but it was her greatest wish that the rest was for the Iroqouis Hounds to continue hunting over. This was an act which was so typical of someone whose influence was almost as immense in death as it had been in life. She became a regular attender of services held at the church and it is the place where Winifred Mooris was laid to rest in her 93rd year.

Before we describe the most unusual happenings, it may be helpful for me to give you a brief introduction to the Iroquois and their most sporting quarry, the coyote.

This is a Hunt which is situated in and around Lexington, Kentucky where the horse rules supreme and thoroughbred farms are prominent throughout. It is also cattle country with large herds of suckler cows being very much part of the farming tradition of the area. The hunt is approximately twenty miles square with rolling blue grass and approximately twenty percent of it woodland. The obstacles vary from wooden coops to rock wall fences. There is however one fact about this interesting and beautiful place to go hunting and that is,

although some red and grey foxes exist, there are very few. This is largely the home of the coyote, and it is he that is at the top of the food chain here, not the fox as it is in most of the UK. He is described by long term Joint Master, Jerry Miller, as the 'King of the Hill'. When it comes to hunting them it appears they will never cease to amaze you.

However the behaviour of this animal is somewhat different and with the experience Lilla has behind her, it not only puts her in a good place to be able to hunt them successfully but most important keep their numbers in balance. I am most grateful to her and Jerry for being kind enough to share with me their knowledge about these indigenous predators. This will help us enormously in understanding more about them before we hear about the extraordinary day's hunting that took place.

According to Lilla the average weight of a coyote is about 74lb, making it approximately 45lb larger than a big dog fox. Unlike the fox, though, they are an animal which does not fight. Each year the male will go out to actively find the same female as the year before, however they do not necessarily live together except for the six week period of the year that the female comes into season. Whilst not cohabitating, they are apparently always on the move and very often are seen travelling in groups which can make the work of the huntsman incredibly difficult when it comes to splitting them. This is also the time when you may well witness the male enticing hounds away from his mate seemingly by being intentionally visible whilst she more than likely will head towards one of the Hunt's good coverts. They also, unlike the vulpine species, very rarely go to ground, and are apt to run fast and straight for many miles.

The Iroquois starts in early October and hunts three days a week right through until April. It can be demanding on horse, hound and humans as the pace is normally considerable. On this occasion however, everything seemed very different. No one person could believe what happened from start to finish and more than a shiver went down the spines of many.

It was a tough call to know whether to hunt or not but it was felt that if anybody would have wanted the Iroqouis Hounds to be hunting on the day of her funeral it would have been Winifred Mooris. So that was decided upon and the Meet moved appropriately to an area five miles or so further north of the country to accommodate all the arrangements being made.

It wasn't long before they found their coyote, and hounds settled down to hunt well. However it was not a racing hunt in the open as is so often the case. On this occasion their quarry seemed to want to stick to the heavily wooded limestone cliffs and creeks which luckily enough are easily crossable because of their rock bottoms. The hunt continued generally in a southerly direction and after approximately ninety minutes, hounds arrived at a covert called Ed Archers Draw, which is a tributary to Boons Creek. Running on from west to east to where the east end of the Draw is intersected by the Grimes Mill Road, the coyote did something very unusual. He ran the road for at least an eighth of a mile right up to St Hubert's Church and the hounds arrived in full voice just as Winifred Mooris's funeral service was well underway. We have now reached the point when it is more appropriate for me to hand over to Lilla, who in her own words can describe exactly what happened next.

"There is a cemetery at the back of the church and to get there one would walk round the south side of the building down a long tree lined alley. At the end of the alley is the statue of Christ with open arms, and that marks the entrance to the cemetery garden. Hounds took exactly that path then stopped just before getting to the statue. They paused, lifted their heads and came back to me – silent".

Herbert Norman

First Whipper In and Kennel Huntsman Cottesmore

Herbert Norman was undoubtedly one of the most popular hunt servants ever to have served the Cottesmore Hunt. He was at the time reputed to be the finest horseman to cross this country, and had worked at the Belvoir under Ben Capell during the Mastership of Sir Gilbert Greenall during 1906.

Herbert served as Second Whipper In during the 1930s to Major C Hilton-Green at the Cottesmore, becoming First Whipper In and Kennel Huntsman (KH) in 1938, continuing during the War. He was very popular amongst the farming community being a great ambassador for hunting in the Cottesmore country. He continued after the War whipping in to Lt Col Cyril Heber-Percy and Sir Henry Tate. His son John started as second horseman in 1932 and

Andrew Osborne and the Cottesmore Hounds

became Second Whipper In in 1937, returning after the War in which he served with great gallantry in bomb disposal. John took over as First Whipper In and K.H. from his father in 1953 when Herbert took his own life. There had been a very severe attack of hardpad and distemper in the kennel and Herbert became very depressed to the extent that he could no longer cope. It is these circumstances that lead to the extraordinary story that I now relate.

In 1956 I came to the Cottesmore as Second Whipper In serving under Lt Col Heber-Percy and Sir Henry Tate. John Norman was then in his third season as 1st Whipper In and K.H. with Harvey Morris as Kennelman. Harvey had been at the Belvoir during the War serving under George Tongue as Whipper In and Kennelman.

In my second season Sir Henry Tate retired from hunting the doghounds, John Norman replaced him as huntsman and I became 1st Whipper In on Thursdays. 1958 saw the retirement of both Col Heber-Percy and Sir Henry Tate from the Mastership of the Cottesmore and Major Bob Hoare came from the West Norfolk and hunted both packs (doghounds and bitches).

Now, to the strange event. Unfortunately I did not keep a hunting diary in those days, so I am not certain of the exact date. It must have been Major Hoare's second season, and the Meet was at Barleythorpe, near Oakham. We found almost at once in the rhododendrons close by the Hall and scent was fair. Hounds ran towards Langham then swung towards the railway line which they crossed leaving Springfield on their right and turned towards the kennels. By this time I had crossed the line at Langham crossing and found myself alone with hounds which ran alongside the line up to the huntsman's house at the kennels, where they checked. I was anxious in case a train came along with hounds trying to pick up a line. Harvey Morris had heard the commotion as the rest of the hounds had started up on hearing the pack. Harvey climbed over the fence and crossed the line whilst I cheered hounds on to him. They duly picked the line up over the railway and away they went, just as the huntsman and field came along the Oakham-Ashwell road. Hounds ran on to Langham and to Ranksborough Gorse then to ground. The strange part of the story is this: Harvey Morris was a great friend of Herbert Norman and talking to him in the valeting room that evening he told me that where hounds checked by the huntsman's house was the exact spot that Herbert took his own life with a .410 shotgun. Not only that, we heard it on good authority that hounds ran on from there through Langham Churchyard right over Herbert's grave!

Another strange thing happened to my wife and me in the Whipper In's cottage at the kennels. My wife is quite certain that she woke in the middle of one night and saw a man standing at the foot of the bed. She said that she told him to "Get out" and he promptly disappeared, which of course woke me up. She swears this happened. I didn't see anything and it never occurred again. Harvey said that since he had been at the kennels no one who had lived there had ever said they had heard or seen anything. However, there had been someone there years ago who had died of anthrax.

There it is though, there are so many things that defy explanation. As St. Paul said: "Now, we see through a glass darkly, but there will come a time when all will be revealed."

Captain Ronald Eden Wallace MFH

23rd July 1919 – 7th February 2002

Ronald Eden Wallace (Ronnie) was born on 23rd July 1919 in the Weald of Kent, his father being Secretary to the Eridge at the time. This was where he grew up and his first skills of becoming a huntsman, for which he was to become famous, were developed. He started with a bobbery pack which included a golden retriever and various other assortments which he collected to hunt the local rabbit population. At the age of eleven he had already got the taste for hunting a fox with his motley crew and made it clear in the Wallace way that this was going to be where his future lay. Learning a lot from Will Freeman (brother to the legendary Frank at the Pytchley) who was hunting the Eridge he soon made substantial progress towards achieving his final goal.

Educated at Eton, along with my father and others whipping-in to him, he soon set about putting the beagles on the map and it is believed that in his last season he accounted for 75 brace of hares and a few foxes as well.

On moving to Gloucestershire the family hunted with the Cotswold, but it was not going to be long before the Wallace enthusiasm for the chase was to be further unleashed. There will be many who have followed his charted course over the years, however a resumé of the packs he hunted and a little more about this talented individual may be of some interest.

In 1938 he went to Christchurch College Oxford. While studying here he took on the Mastership of the Beagles for a while before volunteering for the Army and being commissioned into the Royal Gloucestershire Hussars. While at Sandhurst he formed a private pack of beagles which kept him and other

L-R The Earl of Yarborough MFH, Mr Arthur Lockwood MFH and Capt RE Wallace MFH

Photograph by Jim Meads

potential Officers occupied when not on Military duty. In 1941 it was recorded that he managed sixty two days hunting from Shropshire to Norfolk where he had formed another private pack of beagles to hunt the marshes around Kings Lynn. He thought this part of the world was one of the better scenting parts of the country where he undoubtedly showed good sport. Following a posting as Paymaster to a Prisoner of War Camp at Ludlow, it again did not take him very long to secure the Mastership of the Ludlow Hounds. While hunting them he also managed somehow to secure the time and finance to hunt the adjoining Teme Valley and, during the summer months, the Hawkstone Otter Hounds which he took over from his father in 1946. So as we can see, absolutely no time was wasted in engaging his passion for the chase.

In 1948 he moved to the Cotswolds and there he was soon into his stride and showing excellent sport. However it was not very long before the prying eyes of the Heythrop began to observe his successes. His organisational skills were another aspect for which he was becoming noted, and there was much more. The natural affiliation that Ronnie Wallace was fortunate to have with his hounds and the affection they had for him was quite remarkable. His ability to get the best out of them without any shouting or cracking of whips had to be seen to be believed. All this, combined with a sixth sense about any of the quarry he hunted, made a day hunting a fox, hare or otter run like clockwork. After four seasons here it seemed inevitable that the Heythrop were to get their way and were to benefit for the next twenty five years from his ever growing experience.

In fact hunting overall benefited from his abilities and those did not only lie in the catching of the fox. He was able to walk the corridors of power and seemed to have the knack of having a word with just the right person to ensure something that needed doing was acted upon. This reminds me of how he managed to organise briefings for drivers on the South West rail network, if they should happen to see a pack of hounds on or approaching the line. It would either mean slowing up or briefly stopping the train until hounds could be safely extricated off the line with no risk to passengers or train crew. This was to result in a considerable amount of goodwill between the Hunt and Railway staff, which I was lucky enough to inherit whilst helping Stephen Lambert in his time as Master of the Heythrop. All this of course would be impossible to achieve nowadays. The political climate was made somewhat easier from 1979 for a considerable time but he would never have missed a beat in reminding them just how important hunting was to the countryside. Unfortunately this became more difficult as time progressed as the resentment built up after many years of Conservative Government became clear. Much as the Wallace way had been greatly valued we were heading fast into a different era and one which we know has been doubly difficult with which to deal.

His time at the Heythrop came to an end in 1978 when he moved to Exmoor with Rosie and his son David to live at Mounsey. Exmoor was a place they knew well from their many visits there with the Heythrop hounds in the Spring and it was here that he was to spend the rest of his life, firstly sharing the hunting of the hounds with his Joint Master Jack Hosegood and latterly with his First Whipper In and Kennel Huntsman Tony Wright before finally taking to the car.

Ronnie was served by many great Hunt Staff over the years and the standards that every single one of them set is something of which they should all have been extremely proud. It would be the height of rudeness for me to mention them by name and then omit someone of great importance, but those who are still with us today know exactly who they are. What a difference their contribution made to the success of this extraordinary character who, at the time of his death, had knocked up fifty eight consecutive seasons as a Master. As a result the Wallace name continues to live on.

I therefore think it is fitting to hand over to Tony Wright who was hunting the hounds exactly a year after the Captain's death when a very strange incident occurred. It is he and only he that can tell the story as it happened.

"On Wednesday 6th February 2002 the Exmoor Foxhounds met at Wellshead, Exford by kind invitation of Mr and Mrs Mike Lantz. The weather during the night had been wet and rough, but the day dawned dry with a stiff, westerly wind blowing. I brought 19 couple of Captain Ronnie Wallace's bitch pack to the meet and the Captain was out in his car. He'd been retired from hunting his hounds for five seasons, but if he wasn't following hounds on a horse he would almost certainly be out in a vehicle. Despite the typical Exmoor weather foxes were found nearby and the bitches enjoyed a good scenting day, covering a large area, finishing at 4.40 pm near to Simonsbath having caught a brace.

"The following morning Captain Wallace rang the kennels to speak to me. He was pleased we'd had a good day, and he questioned me about a successful cast he'd spotted which I had made to get hounds beyond a large number of sheep late in the afternoon. I wasn't to realise that this would be the last conversation I would have with him. Later that day Captain Wallace was killed in a car crash on his way to see his wife, Rosie, who was poorly in a Taunton Hospital.

"The next season the Exmoor Foxhounds met on Friday 7th February 2003 to commemorate Captain Wallace's death. The meet was kindly hosted by Miss Pauline Copp, whose home is a short distance from St Luke's Church, Simonsbath where the Captain had been laid to rest. Conditions at dawn were wet and very misty but the drab weather cheered up in time for the meet at 11 am. Once the formalities had taken place the bitch pack was quickly in action opposite the council houses and, although the fox wasn't viewed, hounds ran swiftly straight back to the road at the meet. None of the remaining people there had seen a fox but hounds picked up the line just beyond and hunted away through Cloven Rocks, over the road and into the Exe Valley at Warren Gate. For nearly an hour the bitches hunted on a useful scent, slowly at times through sheep but swiftly on clean ground all about the Pinfords, Warren and Prayway. Finally they brought the line up Three Combes Hill Cleave opposite Warren farm, hunted steadily through sheep foil past the starting point near the meet, and over the wall into the corner of St. Luke's Churchyard at the location of Captain Wallace's grave. They hunted slowly on into the bottom of Ashcombe but here the line was lost. I am not aware that the hunted fox was viewed at any stage of the hunt.

"Hounds were taken to Limecombe Cottage where they found and went away down to Simonsbath Barton. The bitches continued at pace close to Westgate Cottages, on over the Duredon lane, across through the kennels field at Balewater, climbed out and caught a fox just above Duredon farm. With little delay hounds were running again, went up Long Run, through Tangs Bottom, over Top Hill, through Short Chains and Long Chains Combes and straight over the edge of the Chains past the Hoar Oak Buildings. They continued all down the water to Old Scoresdown, up beside the lane rutted to Cheriton farm and out onto Cheriton Ridge. From here they crossed the water to South Furzehill and the Folly, climbed up Ruckham and Thorn Hill to race along the northern edge of the Chains to a proper conclusion below Gammons Corner. A slick performance from Captain Wallace's bitch pack to end the day with a hunt that included a four and a half mile point".

Michael Richard Farrin

1943 – 2008

Huntsman to the Quorn 1968 -1998

Michael Richard Farrin was born in to a farming family in the Atherstone country on 9th February 1943. He was the eldest of five children from Dick and Peggy Farrin. The legendary Captain Parry was Master and with a well-bred pack of hounds on the doorstep it wasn't going to be long before hunting was to become Michael's passion. This was probably in no small part due to the experience he was fortunate enough to have had when he was just eight years old. He was ploughing a field one day for his father when he saw what looked like a rather well hunted fox running down the hedge side in front of him. It wasn't long before the Atherstone Hounds were there in full cry and going like the wind. Michael leapt from his tractor, ran back to the yard, tacked up his pony and in no time was up with them and in hot pursuit. At the end of the Hunt he came home, put the pony away and returned to his plough, only to find the tractor still running. What a wonderful introduction to the Chase for somebody who later in life was to become one of the finest Huntsmen in England. It probably also demonstrated that farm work was not necessarily going to be his forte.

Captain Parry offered Michael the position of Second Horseman at the age of sixteen which he gladly accepted. This was just the beginning of what was going to be a long and illustrious career in Hunt Service. When the Captain moved to the North Cotswold Michael went with him and on this occasion he was promoted to Second Whipper In. He had obviously made a very solid start to his career as in 1963 at just twenty years old he found himself being offered the position as First Whipper In to Jack Littleworth at the Quorn, a job that no man could possibly refuse. Only five years later Jack Littleworth was forced to retire due to failing health so the Masters were faced with the dilemma of who was going to hunt the Quorn Hounds the following season. Were they going to go for someone of a more senior nature or take the risk of promoting Michael who was only twenty five at the time? Well,

Photograph by Jim Meads

The Young Michael Farrin

the decision they made was without doubt the right one. For the next thirty years he dedicated himself whole-heartedly to the Quorn Hounds and the Quorn country, not only as the true professional that he was, but in a way which was totally selfless and very much a hallmark of this great man.

The standard of sport shown during this time was described by many as some of the highest to be found anywhere. His ability to cross Leicestershire in front of such large and notable fields with such ease was proof enough of what a first class and confident horseman he was. He was also one of that rare breed of men who possessed the golden thread with his hounds which makes it all work and is such a joy to watch.

In 1990 after many years at Pawdy Cross Roads, it was decided that new kennels were to be built at Gaddesby Lane, Kirkby Bellars. On arriving for a site meeting one day Michael was more than surprised to see a rather large fox sitting on the very spot where his house was to be built. Throughout the whole time construction work was taking place and well on after the hounds moved in, this particular fox was resident. There was no budging him. You could build new kennels, move the Quorn hounds in but he was going precisely nowhere. It was his territory and that was that. He stayed there for several years and to this day nobody knows quite what became of him.

Michael retired in 1998 after thirty seasons at the very top of his profession. He was going as well at the end of his last as he was his first, but sadly as is the way with a considerable number of hunts there are those who become restless and feel that change is necessary, whether it is going to be for the good of the Hunt or not. So a new career beckoned and this time it was racing that was to benefit from his expertise. He became a dope testing technician and whilst having many friends in the industry, this was a life far away from what Michael had been used to. However the great understanding he was lucky enough to have of horses made sure that his new role was nothing but a success. I was indeed privileged to know Michael really quite well and I was very aware how much he missed his hounds which he had so carefully bred and cared for. I was lucky enough to have heard first hand about the wonderful hunts he had experienced over the years and it was a real pleasure to listen to him recounting them. When I joined the Cottesmore Mastership in 1999 it seemed entirely natural that I should invite Michael to hunt my horses for me in his spare time. He always seemed to be in the right place to see a fox and crossed the country with the same considerable ease that he had done only the season before just over the border. This time however it was on horses that were much more designed for a heavyweight than for him.

Michael stayed in touch over the years and did much to support our family after my wife's accident. However, tragically his own life was to be cut short after being diagnosed with cancer. I called to see him one day but by that time it was in the advanced stages and he died a fortnight later on 18th May 2008. He had put up a tremendous fight for some considerable time but it had beaten him. Whether we hunted on the plough or on the grass hunting had lost a true professional and a great friend. His funeral service took place at St Peters Roman Catholic Church in Melton Mowbray and what a true Huntsman's send off he was given.

The day after Michael's funeral I needed to go to Leicester and had just driven through Melton Mowbray. I was only a quarter of a mile from Kirkby Gate where the Quorn had held their Opening Meet for years and not a mile from the Kennels when, there standing in the middle of the main road, was a very large fox. He had come down from the fields below the Kennels and was heading in the general direction of Frisby on the Wreake, the very village where Michael and Di had retired to, nine years previously. As if this were not strange enough to see at 2.30 pm in the afternoon, later that evening Joanna, Michael's step daughter, was walking her dog up at Cream Gorse which is very close by and one of the Quorn's most famous coverts. It was at approximately the same time of day when she too was confronted by a very large fox, which stood just outside the wood and stared straight at her. He seemed transfixed on Joanna and her dog for some few minutes before trotting away back to the covert and was gone. I had never seen a fox before or since on that particular stretch of road and for those two incidents to have taken place within forty eight hours of Michael being buried sent a shiver down the spine like you would never believe.

Was this a descendant of the old boy who decided to live his life in such close proximity to Michael and his Hounds? We shall never know, but there is one thing we can say and that is, it was more than likely so.

Here are a few lines from a poem which was read at Michael's funeral. I think you will agree it is not only an appropriate tribute to the abilities of this most modest of men but also is one from him to those wonderful Quorn bitches of which he was justly proud.

An Extract from Forty Fine Ladies

By Patrick R Chalmers

Out to a party go forty fine ladies
Forty fine ladies when noon tide is grey,
Light on their feet where the glade is,
Sweet are their tongues on the wet winter's day.

Forty fine ladies, the queens of the revel,
Forty fine ladies, so lashing and level,
Forty fine ladies, who'll dance like the devil
Race like a smoke wreath away.

Forty fine ladies, they found in their ballroom,
Such a shy gallant, eight miles he had come,
Chased him and raced him and gave him but small room,
Showed him, the rascal, new reason to roam.

Richard Gilby Teather

1913 – 1983
Terrier Man to the Burton

Richard Gilby (Dick) Teather was one of those rare characters who died in the same village in which he was born, and where he had lived for his full seventy years. This was Hackthorn, in the heart of the Burton country. Dick was a father of three, one son and two daughters, and although he was an engineer, working at Robey's in Lincoln, at heart he was one of the most true and genuine of countrymen you could find.

This story is quite remarkable and took place nearly two years after Dick's death. It is interesting for the fact that these instances do not always occur immediately and can very often happen many years afterwards. I am indebted to Peter, Dick's son, for the details of what you are about to read, and to Jim Lang, former Huntsman to the Burton for helping with added information.

The Burton hounds and the terriers which he worked were, other than his family, Dick's great love and his enthusiasm for the chase was of huge importance to him. For example he would never take family holidays. During cubbing he arranged it so he could hunt in the morning and then work the afternoon shift. Full days would be taken off during the regular season so he could attend to the important duties which were entrusted to him. Initially he started following on a bicycle with one of his home bred Jack Russell's in a box on the front and a spade attached to the cross bar. He then progressed to a motorbike and then to a Morris 8 soft top. While there was a network of good old fashioned earth stoppers in the country at the time, Dick took full responsibility for the Hackthorn area which he knew like the back of his hand. Many a night was spent studying the

country to find where foxes might be and seeing what damage they had been inflicting on the local poultry population. This is a real art and is not all about the stopping of earths. Possessing a deep knowledge of the vulpine species is invaluable in this case and Dick had that in bucket loads. The fox is an animal that never ceases to amaze us so knowing at least something about their habits certainly helps.

You could say Dick Teather fitted into his life as a countryman as a hand into a glove. With no television in the house, Dick was a great reader and was someone who can certainly be described as a true naturalist. He thoroughly enjoyed sharing the things he learnt with all those around him. This also helped the Burton in other ways. It was the time when inter hunt quizzes were popular and with Dick on their team, you could be sure they would normally win or be thereabouts.

As time progressed Dick joined the Hunt Committee with his daughter Sue following him as Hunt Treasurer. She also became Secretary to the Hunt Supporters. With their combined loyalty the Burton benefitted hugely from their efforts. As well as giving so freely of their time, Dick and Sue made sure they always walked a single hound puppy every year. When the time came for hound exercise Huntsman Jim Lang would always make a point of calling in for some much needed refreshments. Their pups from previous years would instantly recognise not only their surroundings but those who had given them a thoroughly good start in life.

Hackthorn of course, had been home since birth for Dick, so he knew everybody in the village and on the estate which at that time belonged to the Amcotts family. When the hounds met at the Hall their Butler Fred Pratt made sure that when Mr Dick Teather appeared at the Meet, a glass of fine port was produced for him rather than the cooking sherry that was made available for everybody else. He was quite obviously a man with immense popularity as this simple gesture goes to show.

In his later years Dick's health began to suffer so Jim continued to ensure that regular visits were made to Hackthorn with the hounds during the summer months. Calling in one day Jim sat underneath the bedroom window chatting away when suddenly Dick's concentration ceased and for the next few minutes he seemed to be totally focused on the hounds. "Now boys and girls, listen carefully to me" he said. "When I return, I will be coming back as a fox and I am going to give you a good hunt and you are going to catch me on the front lawn at Hackthorn Hall." "Don't be daft." replied Jim, and that was all that was said. However, please just take this opportunity to recollect, Dick absolutely adored the hounds he had addressed that morning. He died at home not many months afterwards and has long since been remembered in the Burton country by all who knew him and had such respect for him.

Two years later Jim had gone down with the flu and could not hunt hounds for a short while so Robert Buckland, the First Whipper In, was put on in his absence. The meet on this particular day was at the Brownlow Arms at Faldingworth in the country heading out towards Market Rasen. After a very busy day they found an outlier near Cold Hanworth and flew round by West Firsby, Spridlington and out to Hackthorn. Running up nearly to the main Lincoln to Scunthorpe Road, they turned back and after completing a couple of quick circuits of the village, they caught their fox on the front lawn at Hackthorn Hall.

On arriving back to the Kennels, Jim had extracted himself from his sick bed and managed to put the flesh out in the feed room for his hounds' return. "Well how did you get on?" he enquired. Robert explained where they had been and that they had been busy all day, finishing up with a flier from Cold Hanworth and that they had caught their fox at Hackthorn on the front lawn of the Hall. Jim stood back and for a minute was in total shock at what he had just heard. Then he turned to his Whipper In and said: "Bloody hell Robert, you have just gone and killed Dick!"

Mad March Hares

Colonel John Anthony Cowen
1831 – 1895

For this next piece I am indebted to Joe Cowen of Fernie fame for this most fascinating story about his Great Uncle who was Master of the Braes of Derwent in County Durham. The extraordinary thing about this particular incident is that Colonel Cowen was very seriously ill at the time and was being cared for at his home at Blaydon Burn. He died just a few weeks later on 14th April 1895 and it was from there this whole true story unravelled. Although there are sometimes strange happenings around the time of a death, it is more unusual for them to happen before than afterwards.

Colonel John Anthony Cowen, the second son of Sir Joseph Cowen, was born at Blaydon Burn House in 1831. He was described as a handsome young man with a beard and moustache and penetrating blue eyes. He was universally popular wherever he went in County Durham and was a great participant of the manly sports of England, be it hunting, shooting, fishing or hawking. He was held in high esteem by his industrial employees at Blaydon and Blaydon Burn and was also extremely well respected for his fair dealing as a JP on the Gateshead Bench. He married Isabella Lilley Atkin from Benwell, at that time a small village just two miles west of Newcastle.

In days that were far less democratic than they are today farmers, puppy walkers, earth stoppers and members of the Hunt would mix freely at the numerous functions that the Hunt held. Colonel Cowen also enjoyed entertaining his friends at home as well as giving his Hunt Supporters a dinner at Riding Mill in the Tyne Valley. Although he was a temperate man himself he loved to ensure his friends were well fed and watered. The Meets at Blaydon Burn were, it is believed, most popular events.

The season of 1894/1895 was marred by the Colonel lying seriously ill at home. Towards the end of the season the hounds met at the village of Ryton on 9th March. Having found at Bewes Hills Whin hounds ran well to Blaydon Burn. They checked in the Kennel fields and then ran on into the garden where Miss Mary Cowen, his daughter who had been looking after him, viewed the fox from the windows of the house. After much excitement in and around the outbuildings and shrubberies the fox was caught on the lawn in full view of the Colonel who had witnessed the entire proceedings from a chair in his bedroom. This was the last time that Colonel Cowen saw the Braes of Derwent hounds of which he had been Master of for twenty three seasons.

On 2nd December 1938 Mr John Cowen, the Colonel's son, who had been Secretary to the Braes of Derwent for thirty eight seasons, died at Minsteracres in the Newcastle and District Beagles country. Almost a month later their New Year's Day Meet was held at Healey and it wasn't very long before they found their first hare. She decided not only to go back to Healey Churchyard but straight to the place where Mr Cowen had been buried just those few weeks before. It was said afterwards that as the beagles ran straight over the top of his grave they gave of their very best with a real merry cry.

There are two unusual aspects to these stories. First I am of the belief that it is somewhat out of the ordinary for foxes in particular to do something before a death is announced, although not unheard of. Second, although hares are mysterious animals it is somewhat rare to hear of such an incident as the above involving one of them.

OBITUARIES

Clarence Webster

1928 - 2008

Although Clarence Arthur Webster died seven years ago, I was privileged along with Chairman Green, Master of the Warwickshire, to write his obituary for Horse and Hound. 'Clarrie' as we fondly knew him left his mark on a very large number of people and many of us can still imagine his smiling face. It is therefore in his honour that we reproduce the obituary, which was the first to go on the For the Love of Hunting England website. It says so much about a family who dedicated their lives to hunting.

Clarence Arthur Webster, or 'Clarrie' as he was affectionately known, died earlier this year and was well known as one of the finest examples of professional Huntsmen, who not only dedicated his life to his hounds, but to showing a high standard of sport as well. Clarrie was undoubtedly bred for the job, his grandfather and great grandfather also having been in Hunt Service. He was born at the Essex Union Kennels in 1928 where his father, also Arthur, was Huntsman and it was not to be long before the young Webster was in action. With war being declared he was seconded into whipping in, whilst his brother Jim, who went on to hunt the Belvoir, was already on active service with the Tank Regiment in Northern France. It was at the time of the bombing of London that the kennels were badly damaged one evening, by a Doodle Bug, which had over shot its mark. However in typical Webster fashion everything was cleared up without a fuss and the hounds were hacked on the following morning as though nothing had happened, arriving a fraction late for the 11.00 o'clock meet. Colonel Heatley who had been waiting for them enquired of Arthur Webster as to why they were late. The reply came that a bomb had fallen on the kennels during the night. The Colonel was overheard in reply, by Clarrie, to say: "What the dickens are you doing here at all then?"

The Essex Union at that time was a real sporting country, being all grass. It would therefore have been a great place to learn the trade, especially as after a spell with the Royal Horse Artillery, the young Webster was put on to whip in to the Wynnstay, under the well respected disciplinarian, Jack Simister. It was here he was to meet his future wife Ennis, whose kind and caring nature not only ensured the smooth running of the Webster household, but that of the role of a Huntsman's wife, which Ennis was to fit admirably. After three seasons

Photograph by Jim Meads

here, George Gillson required a First Whipper In at the Warwickshire. It was here that Clarrie was to spend the rest of his life. When George Gillson left to go to the Meynell, Clarrie was appointed as First Whipper In and Kennel Huntsman to Major Profumo for the following season. As time progressed he was asked to hunt hounds, which he did with great professionalism. As well as being a top class Huntsman, Clarrie was a true ambassador for the sport, knowing his country and its farmers off the back of his hand. He also had great admiration for the fox and many an enjoyable evening was spent with glass of whisky in hand, recounting where hounds had run that day and over whose land they had been. At the same time we must never forget the friendly advice he gave to all of us who worked under him, and whose great ambition it was to hunt a pack of hounds.

After twenty five seasons showing sport to the highest standard, and with the unstinting love and support of Ennis and their son Mark, Clarrie retired to Sutton under Brailes to a cottage kindly provided by Miss Boultbee Brooks, a former Master of the Warwickshire. He still followed the fortunes of the Warwickshire hounds, and quietly gave great assistance and advice to the four Huntsmen who succeeded him: Anthony Adams, Ralph Mankee, William Deakin and John Pritchard. After retirement from Hunt Service, Clarrie worked for members of the Sewell family where he became very much part of their family. He took great pride in his garden and in helping many others in the village, whatever the task. Clarrie will be much missed for many reasons but most of all for his distinctive Webster smile, and his cheerful whistle, which his hounds adored him for.

Elizabeth Jane Cecil Hill

26th February 1925 - 25th August 2013

Elizabeth Jane Cecil Hill was born at Lynchmere near Guildford into a non-hunting family. Jane's father was a Naval Commander who after the War went on to become an engineer with Rolls Royce. Whilst Jane's mother's maiden name was Purkis, a well-known sporting name in the New Forest going back many generations, it would appear however that neither family had any previous involvement in the chase. This though was all set to change when the activities of both horse and hound entered into Jane's life and it was hunting that certainly brought her a huge amount of satisfaction and pleasure in the coming years.

Jane initially trained as a radiologist at the Middlesex Hospital before moving down to Boscombe in Dorset. While she was working in Bournemouth Hospital Jane met Ralph Hill, a government scientist who designed radios for the army. The bug must have bitten and with memories of being taught as a child to ride by the Kings Trainer, it was not long before hunting and a little point to pointing was to take hold. In 1958 Ralph was to become Joint Master of the New Forest Foxhounds, initially with Col. and Mrs East and then with Bridget Scott who went on to join probably one of our country's most knowledgeable hound breeders, Sir Newton Rycroft. In 1962 Ralph, although relinquishing his duties as a Joint Master, carried on as Field Master to Sir Newton who, in his own particular style, was making a real success of hunting the hounds. Then in 1973 Jane became Hunt Secretary, a role she much enjoyed and at which she was extremely good.

During her busy life Jane most successfully brought up five sons, Peter, John, Nicholas, Mark, and Oliver as well as walking numerous foxhound and beagle puppies. The hunting gene, it would appear, seemed to come out most strongly in Mark and Oliver with both of them devoting their lives to the sport in a most considerable and meaningful way. While Mark was Master of the Marlborough College Beagles he would often bring them back home to Burley for the holidays and was known to venture as far as Hertfordshire and Essex in pursuit of the hare.

Whilst serving her term as Secretary Jane became immensely popular with those who lived and worked in the New Forest, especially the Keepers who thought the world of her. Graham Wilson, one of the more senior, said there was great mutual respect for each other. As well as this, they equally shared a

Jane Hill with her husband Ralph, former Master of the New Forest

Photograph by Jim Meads

passion for the Forest, its traditions and hunting of course, be it with the Foxhounds or the Buckhounds, was very much part of this. When Jane became unable to drive, it was wonderful that they ensured she was still able to follow her beloved New Forest hounds. This was something the family will never forget and for which they will always be indebted to them. To see them represented at her Memorial Service with Graham Wilson in Forest Livery, summed up the feelings of the New Forest Keepers for this wonderful lady in a most memorable and moving way.

Last and by no means least, we must never forget the sense of duty Jane felt towards her home village of Burley. Whether it was delivering Meals on Wheels, driving for the over seventies or just for being the most wonderful mother, Jane could always be relied on, if ever help or support were needed. So in her passing we remember her for being one of the very best examples of a truly Christian lady. She was someone who served her community in a way that only Elizabeth Jane Cecil Hill knew, and that was always to put others first. I am sure there are many who will agree from Burley and in many other parts of the New Forest that it was a real privilege to have known her. Elizabeth Jane Hill's commitment to us all will remain long in our memories.

Major Eric Comerford

1915 - 2009

Major Eric Comerford was born in February 1915 at Deene House, Caxton in the Cambridgeshire country, one of three sons and two daughters. With the Kennels in the same village and a mother and father who were both enthusiastic foxhunters, a life revolving around hunting seemed most likely. How true this was to be. Eric's childhood was spent in school at Blackfriars, near Stamford and in his spare time he and his family would be out with the Cambridgeshire, either hacking long distances to meets or putting their horses and ponies on the train to go further afield. With a pack of Foxhounds in the close vicinity and a 600 acre wood nearby, what more could they have wished for.

Fitzwilliam Benson

Much of Eric's early working life was spent in Sussex and Leicestershire, breaking and hunting young horses. To be out with the Fernie behind the legendary Bert Peaker, as well as having many days with Major Hilton Green at the Cottesmore, Sir Harold Nutting at the Quorn and Lord Daresbury at the Belvoir must have been the highlight of any young person's life. This was at the time when the Shires were, without any doubt, at their best and these days were to last long in Eric's memory. Moving to the Woodland Pytchley country, Eric married Jessie in October 1939 and went on to join the 52nd Heavy Regiment (Bedfordshire Yeomanry). As War broke out he was commissioned into the Royal Artillery, with whom he saw active service throughout Europe. It was in 1942 whilst Eric was in combat that his son Bill was born.

With the War over, things began to return to normal. Life was based very much around farming and hunting. This could not have been more suitable for somebody with Eric's upbringing. For a while he farmed a herd of Guernsey cattle in the Pytchley country at Harrington. As well as working in the grain trade, Eric still made time to hunt at least one day a week. This was a must and certainly had to be achieved, as the Pytchley hounds were in tremendous form at the time, showing the best of sport. What more was one to expect, when the Master was Colonel Lowther and the Huntsman none other than the great Stanley Barker. The opportunity was one not to be missed and was a true hunting man's dream. This was another most memorable part of Eric's life.

After a move back to the Woodland Pytchley country, Eric and Jessie continued to farm, this time at Pipewell. In 1970 he took on the Joint Mastership with Captain Chris Thursfield, on Pat Escombe's retirement. He stayed at the Woodland Pytchley country, which was his favourite, for the next 14 seasons. He really made his mark, and when the Major spoke everybody immediately knew that it was not only a voice that had to be listened to, but immediately taken notice of. He was extremely popular amongst the farmers within the country and there was hardly a blade of grass that he did not know. He was extremely lucky with his Huntsmen during this time and they included Cooper Atkinson who went on to hunt the Brocklesby, Tom Teanby who later hunted the Fitzwilliam (Milton) but sadly died in office, and Lindsay Hall who is currently hunting the Barlow.

When Jessie became ill he cared for her right to the end, which sadly came in 1982. They had been married for 43 years. Eric then came to live in the Fitzwilliam country in 1987. He became immensely popular and gave great support to the Mastership of Sir Stephen and the Hon Lady Hastings, Sir Phillip Naylor Leyland, and James Barclay. If ever anybody was to be in the right place at the right time to either see the fox away or when hounds were struggling, it would be Eric on his old horse Ginger. The combined age of the pair of them came to a goodly number of years. He was a wonderful source of good advice to those of us at the sharp end, about how to run a hunting country. It was always most gratefully received and more often than not was accompanied by a rather large glass of whisky. Many great birthday meets were held in his honour at Chapel End, Great Gidding, right up unto his 90th, with his good friends from far and wide in attendance.

We will all remember Eric for many different reasons and those of us who knew him will miss him greatly. He was very much a gentleman of the old school, and the country is certainly, without any doubt whatsoever, by far the poorer for his passing.

Peter Needham

1923 - 2014

In large areas of Lincolnshire and beyond the name Needham is very well known and respected, especially in the worlds of farming and foxhunting. However, if you are somebody who is involved with both these activities and you hear Peter being mentioned, you will instantly see in your mind's eye his wonderful smiling face, which over many years epitomised his enthusiasm and love of hunting.

Peter was born at Rookery Farm, Great Hale on the Blankney - Belvoir borders on the 13th September 1923, to Percy and Marjorie. He was one of six, three boys and three girls, with Peter being the second child. He and his brother John took to the chase when old enough, hacking long distances to meets of the Blankney. Their early days were spent learning how to plough and roll with heavy horses and Peter obtained his first pony at the age of eight. This was the very beginning of the love and passion he developed for the horse and it was one which stayed with him right until the end of his life. Peter did not enjoy education, preferring to be outdoors, so as a result Sleaford Grammar School probably saw little of him when farming duties took

Peter Needham MFH out with the Blankney

over or even perhaps if the hounds were in the area. Many of his generation probably learnt more about life by joining the local Young Farmers Club and Peter was no different. He found himself deeply involved and it was with his input that they went on to win many cups over the years. Whilst enjoying the life of a Young Farmer like so many, he went on and found the girl of his dreams, Jean. She later became very popular and suitably impressed him by winning first prize for plucking and drawing a bird, a very useful skill to have in those days and one not many of the young would be that keen on today. Jean and Peter were married in 1952 and went on to have two children, Helen and Gerald and whilst busy bringing them up, they engrossed themselves in a life of farming, breeding horses and of course, the Blankney hounds.

The hunting bug really started to bite when Peter was in his early twenties and this resulted from meeting a well-known horse dealer called Ted Dudley. From then on, whilst continuing to farm, the challenge of trying out young fiery horses really started to take hold, being more than keen to undertake this for their neighbour, a Miss Barbara Godson. He was, as many have told me, totally fearless. Although not on a horse at his last Blankney Opening Meet, his enthusiasm was still as strong as ever. Peter served on the Hunt Committee for well over forty years, as well as being on the Point to Point and Hunt Supporters Committees for more years than one could mention. However it was his stints as Master, firstly with Ruth Parker and latterly Margaret Morris where he really left his mark. His popularity amongst the farming community of Lincolnshire was earned through his dedication and attention to detail, and as a result ensured the best access to the very large majority of farms in the Blankney country. Although Peter hunted hounds when George Knight and Jack Deakin were laid up, it was an ambition that sadly he never fulfilled to his overall satisfaction. However as we all know he made up for it in so many different ways, not least in encouraging his grandchildren and taking them on with him, so they could get a view of the hunted fox stealing its way across the Heath. His legendary holloa is something they and many others will never forget.

Peter and Jean were well known throughout the land and they loved visiting other parts of the country to hunt, particularly the Cotswolds. He never failed to enthuse all of us who had the privilege of knowing him in the pleasures that hunting and a rural life could bring. He will be remembered for his kindness, his generosity of spirit and most importantly as a very fine example of a proper countryman. Lincolnshire and the hunting world have lost one of the best that the county could produce.

Peter, may the foxes in heaven give you the pleasure they did down here and may they run straight and far as was the case in your heyday when the Blankney hounds were in full cry behind them.

John Cooke – "Cookie"
1930 - 2013

John Cooke (Cookie) was born on 14th November 1930 at Revesby Park in Lincolnshire, his father John Herbert Cooke being Stud Groom to Lady Beryl Groves. On leaving school at fourteen Cookie went to work at an auctioneer's office. This certainly was not his scene and he moved swiftly on to the South Wold (West) Kennels as general factotum which was much more his cup of tea. The South Wold had been split into two and the well respected Mr Leslie Butcher was Master with the hounds being kennelled at his home at Edlington on the edge of the Lincolnshire Wolds. Cookie started to learn the groundwork of kennel life which was later to prove invaluable to him, as he developed his own very high standards. After four seasons he took up his National Service with the Kings Troop Royal Horse Artillery, then progressed to whip in to the Linlithgow and Stirlingshire, the nearby Burton and Newmarket and Thurlow, where eldest son Jonathan was born. From here

The South Wold hounds at home

he went to the Wilton near Salisbury, with his next stop being the Meynell, in Staffordshire under one of the best known huntsmen of that time, George Gillson, who was born at the South Wold Kennels, at Belchford.

Whilst at the Meynell Cookie became known by Mr Gillson as Jack for some unknown reason. This must have been about the time when his sense of humour was really beginning to develop, for if he had done something that was not quite to Mr. Gillson's satisfaction he would start mimicking him. "Come now Jack, come now", he would say. "Hold them with your eyes not your whip." Hound exercise at the Meynell was strenuous enough in itself, the hounds leaving the Kennels at seven in the morning, very often not being back till three in the afternoon. During one of these long jaunts he was once offered a piece of cake with a cup of tea. Apparently he was so hungry that his belly button was nearly touching his backbone but he dare not look at the cake. On another occasion Cookie observed a Vulcan Bomber flying over. He enquired of Mr Gillson, "Did you see that plane, Sir?" To which came the reply, "No Jack, are there any foxes or hounds up there?"

Whilst at the Meynell Nicholas, Cookie's youngest son, was born. Shortly after his birth he was held high above the bedroom window sill of the Whipper In's house for all to see as they returned from a lengthy Gillson hound exercise. Cookie was very proud that at seventeen Nicholas took up a career with Sussex Police serving his full thirty year term before retiring.

Cookie left the Meynell to return to the Wilton as Huntsman to Lord Folkestone, where he stayed for four seasons. Whilst he was at the Wilton, Sir Newton Rycroft became a good friend and was a constant source of wise advice. As many of us will remember there was no more fascinating man to learn from than Sir Newton. Early on in his time hunting the Wilton hounds Mr Gillson's words would ring in his ears: "Never lie to your hounds and they will never lie to you, trust them and never kid them." Wonderful words of advice for a young Huntsman. After four successful seasons at the Wilton, it was time for a move to the Eridge, taking over from Brian Gupwell who had just left for Badminton.

John Goode, recently retired Huntsman of the Brocklesby and Martin Thornton, former Huntsman of the Belvoir, both whipped in to Cookie and it undoubtedly gave him great pleasure to think he had played an important part in educating such first class men for the job. Likewise it has to be said, they equally would have been proud to have worked for such a great boss. The Eridge hounds at the time were very good in their work and also of an equally high standard in their looks. As a result there were many occasions on which they gave the Green coats of the Beaufort and Heythrop a run for their money and at a Peterborough bitch championship he found himself sandwiched between them with his Fizzle'73.

In 1980 the Eridge celebrated their centenary and the Duke of Beaufort and Captain Wallace were invited to judge the Puppy Show. All morning was spent shampooing the hounds and everything had gone according to plan until such time it was decided to walk them out when what should appear, but a fox. In a flash they were gone. Eventually they returned looking rather weary and somewhat dirty, Cookie had to turn round and bathe them all again. It was therefore somewhat ironic that the Duke remarked that he thought the Eridge hounds were in rather good voice as he arrived for lunch.

Cookie developed a tremendous rapport with both Molly Gregson of Crawley and Horsham fame and Richard Barlow, the long serving Master of the Chiddingfold and Leconfield since 1936, who oversaw the amalgamation with the Cowdray in 1973. They were obviously most impressed with the standards he kept, coupled with the genial and most polite nature of the man, whose company they much enjoyed.

After thirteen seasons at the Eridge, Cookie returned to his native Lincolnshire which he always looked upon as home. This time it was to hunt the South Wold which, in 1947, had returned to being a single Hunt, the South Wold (West) and the South Wold (East) having come back together, with their hounds kennelled at Belchford, near Horncastle. They were lucky enough to have a strong Mastership of well respected Lincolnshire farmers. This stood them in good stead for the many enjoyable days which were due to follow either high up on the Wolds or down on the Marsh towards the coast.

With his son Jonathan, whom he had originally taught to ride on a donkey, whipping in to him the Cooke duo were now in their element, and as Jonathan explained "Dad certainly didn't suffer fools gladly." This part of the country has changed very little over the years, the only real difference being that the Marsh, which was undoubtedly one of the best grazing places in the country for fattening cattle, has succumbed like so many areas to the plough. However nothing was going to stop Cookie and Jonathan showing the best of sport. The hunt that is probably best remembered from that era is the one from Motherwood, a large and very thick covert not too far from Alford. From here they ran down virtually to the Coast to just north of Skegness, narrowly avoiding the Golden Sands Holiday Park. They then ran back to Castle Carlton where the fox went to ground under a hen house. Pete Hyland, the very well known and respected breeder of terriers, bolted a fresh fox and the hounds disappeared into the dark.

There were many other most exciting days to come, however on the way back from one of them Jonathan and his Father had a narrow escape. They had just started to descend Cawkwell Hill, the steepest hill in the Wolds, when the lorry's brakes failed, with two horses and a pack of hounds on board. Just able to ram it into first gear they managed to find themselves getting to the bottom all in one piece but in some sort of sweat for a while afterwards. I am sure Cookie's expression, "ooh yer bugger" could be heard loud and clear on that occasion.

Cookie retired in 1992 as there was a change in Mastership. He and his wife Shirley then moved to Cornbury Park in the Heythrop country to work for Lord Rotherwick where they walked puppies for both the Heythrop and the Bicester. His abiding interest in the hounds stayed with him until the day he died. Whether it was a preview, a puppy show or a hound show you knew he would be there, wanting to see and expecting the very highest of standards, because it truly mattered to him. Cookie not only knew the breeding of nearly every hound in the Kennels he visited, but every Master as well. Latterly he thoroughly enjoyed his stewarding at Peterborough Royal Foxhound Show.

He and I were invited to judge at the Belvoir one year, during my time at the South Wold. A pal tipped me the wink that something funny was up and sure enough it was. For some unknown reason, Martin Thornton thought it would be a good idea to put a microphone on each of us and asked us to explain to the assembled company what we were looking for whilst judging a hound. Well you can imagine the scene. Here is a rather large over weight Master and a very dapper little fellar with a rose in his button hole, each attached to a microphone. It all turned out to be more like a comedy show than a Puppy Show. "You do the talking, Sir". Then he would make some comical remark which would bring the house down, by saying something like, "Bet they have never done this at Belvoir before."; "What would your Grandfather have to say?"; "Standards aren't what they were, are they, Sir?"

Cookie was a shining example of a true and dedicated Hunt Servant who will be greatly missed by all who knew him. Whether it was his ability to hunt a pack of hounds, his melodious and cheerful voice echoing round the Eridge Woodlands, or how he made us laugh and smile as he blew gone away from the barrels of a twelve bore. Our lives have certainly been enriched by knowing him. It must be unheard of for the last words about an outstanding professional to be left to a hunt saboteur, Mick Camplin, who spent a lot of his time badgering Cookie, but he told Jonathan when they met in Horncastle shortly after Cookie's death had been announced in the local newspaper: "I was so sorry to hear about your Dad, he was a really good bloke."

That is something that the twenty six Masters and Huntsmen from throughout the country who attended Cookie's Memorial Service, as well as the very large congregation, would all agree on.

Jack Deakin
1925 - 2014

Jack Deakin was born on 18th July 1925 at the Tiverton Foxhound Kennels where his father was First Whipper In to Sir Ian Heathcote Amory. Jack was to be the eleventh child out of twelve and with Hunt Service being on both sides of the family, it seemed fairly inevitable this would be where his life would take him. Sure enough it did, not only for him but two of his brothers, Dick, who went on to hunt the Essex Union, Jim the South Tetcott and with Jack finishing up hunting the Blankney for six seasons. After leaving Devon the family moved to the Cumberland where Jack schooled at Aspatria before being signed up as an eighteen year old into the Fleet Air Arm. Sailing out on the Queen Mary to New York he then made his way by train via Alabama to Trinidad where he trained as an aircraft mechanic servicing Mustangs. After the War he decided he wanted to become a jockey. This was not however to be the case and almost immediately he found himself in Hunt Service, starting as Whipper In to Jumbo Wilkinson at the South Durham. After a couple of seasons he made his way to the Essex and Suffolk as Second Whip to Chris Parsons and then on to his first stint at the Newmarket and Thurlow under Charlie Field. Here he was to meet the future Mrs Deakin and marry her, before moving to the Bicester and Warden Hill where the well known disciplinarian Charlie Johnson was hunting hounds, another man who had the blood of hunt service running thick through his veins. Whilst they were at Stratton Audley Mrs Deakin took to hunting on a bicycle with her terrier Panda accompanying her on many occasions.

On being approached to whip in to the well known amateur Huntsman of the South Pembrokeshire, David Harrison Allen, Jack decided this was a positive move to make. They stayed here for four most enjoyable seasons and during their time at Creselly their sons Tony and Barry were born. It was then off to the Belvoir and next back to the Newmarket and Thurlow as Huntsman to their highly respected Master Harvey Leader. A one season move to the Badsworth took place before Jack was offered the position of First Whipper In and

Kennel Huntsman to Mr Bill Cressey at the Rockwood Harriers, where they spent eleven very successful seasons. Their third son Michael was born completing the family and they have many happy memories of this time. Whether it was hunting hounds, whipping in or showing them, Jack had a wonderful talent using a very quiet approach. This worked wonders with Harriers which are prone to be somewhat over excitable. It paid off not only in the field where he had them hunting extremely well for the Major but also on their annual visits to Peterborough where Jack had their total undivided attention. Not only did they win a considerable number of classes over the years, but also a significant collection of championships. This was entirely down to his dedication to them, and the great respect they had for him. This is a fine example of what we describe in the trade, as the golden thread.

During the hard winter of 1962/63 a very strange thing happened at the Rockwood Kennels. Like everything in the wild at the time, foxes were struggling to find enough food to survive, so when one morning Jack tracked a vulpine friend in the snow across the dividing wall between the Rockwood doghounds and the Rockwood bitches and then on into the flesh house he could scarcely believe his eyes. Hunger may have been one thing on this fox's mind, but he knew exactly what he was doing and where he was going.

Jack's final move in Hunt Service was to the Blankney where initially he whipped in to the Rt. Hon James Fitzroy, now Lord Southampton, for one season, before hunting hounds for the next six. The straight necked foxes of Lincolnshire proved an interesting challenge for Jack. The quiet approach he had used with the Harriers paid off with him and the Blankney hounds showing some fine sport over the ensuing years. Eventually however, the time came to retire. His sons were just at the age of enjoying motorbikes, and they told me this rather amusing story about their father. One Sunday morning they sent him off on a bike to see how he got on. He eventually returned back to the Kennels pushing it, telling them in no uncertain terms that it seemed to have a different sort of horse power to what he was used to, and didn't respond to "woah, you b...... thing". Jack's last challenge was to set up a most successful boarding kennel on Blankney Heath. He would bring in dogs with psychological problems from many different places with the Police and the RSPCA being just two of his good customers. The way he had handled his hounds paid off with his new canine friends and those with the worst issues soon found themselves being calmed down and transfixed by Jack in his own distinctive way. A lifetime in Hunt Service had certainly helped him in developing his skills further in retirement and was one that the RSPCA should take seriously.

Jack will long be remembered for his good humour with his laugh lasting long in the memory of his family and many others around him.

The Blankney hounds outside Blankney Church where Jack Deakin's funeral took place

Burton Hounds 7th March 2015

In Memory of David Thomas Todd
5th January 1937 - 2nd May 2015
"Until We Meet Again"

HOW HUNT SERVICE HAS CHANGED IN THE 21ST CENTURY

For hunting to survive it has to constantly change and this is especially true in the role that Hunt Staff play. I thought therefore it would be interesting to have a look at just how much Hunt Service has changed from the 20th to the 21st Century. To enable us to have a clear picture in our mind about the valuable tasks our Hunt Staff perform we need to look back and see just how much things have changed, which they have – dramatically. Sadly we all know about the most significant change but putting that on one side for a moment we must look at the other contributory factors that have altered the overall fabric of such an historical institution. All this is just as important today as it was a hundred years ago.

The seasons running up to the Second World War were in many countries the golden era of foxhunting, and that I believe is a good place to start. The country at the time was unfortunately going through an horrific agricultural depression. There were thousands of acres of uncultivated land which of course ironically made it a foxhunters paradise. There were foxes everywhere the hounds went and there were very few limitations where they could go. Although at this time some politicians may have started thinking about dealing the sport a severe blow, their first attempt was to come four years after the War. Luckily that was to fail, but as we know it was not to be the end of the matter. There were and always have been more important issues with which to deal than banning foxhunting. Even though this is a few years before I was born, I was lucky enough to hear much from my forebears as well as being extremely fortunate to have had access to their hunting diaries.

The Puckeridge, like many at the time, was in its heyday. The country, in spite of its very close proximity to the Capital City, was remarkably wild and the hounds were out four days a week with Bob Gardiner, the professional, hunting the bitches and my grandfather hunting the dog hounds. There were two whippers in, two Kennelmen and numerous staff looking after the hunt horses and the country. Although it always was renowned for being a plough country pack, fields were large and sport was at its best with five, six and seven mile points being regular occurrences.

However the threat of the Germans pushing too far towards Poland was never far away and became reality on 3rd September 1939, the day that War was declared. Whilst there was little action for a while, it wasn't long before many of those who were actively in Hunt Service at the time were seconded to different regiments around the UK and sent out to fight. A very large number returned but inevitably some didn't. For those that were lucky enough to do so, they found in just those few years hunting had changed greatly. In the case of the Puckeridge the size of the pack had been drastically reduced at the very beginning of the War, with a large number of dog hounds being put down. Ben Wilkinson became First Whipper In and Kennel Huntsman on Bob Gardiner's retirement, and he was ably assisted by my Aunt Pamela and Dick Bull as the Kennelman. Feeding humans was a struggle but to find enough to keep a pack of hounds going for the next six seasons was far from easy. However they remained resolute and were there to give the pleasures of the chase to those who returned from the horrors of what was going on in mainland Europe.

The countryside had also changed drastically during and after the war years as the nation needed to concentrate its efforts not only on fighting off the enemy but producing sufficient food. As a result, combined with ever increasing urbanisation, the Puckeridge was unable to return to hunting four days a week, until they amalgamated with the Newmarket and Thurlow in 1970. This would have been an identical problem for the

Hertfordshire, Old Berkeley, and South Oxfordshire Hunts, who in the same year joined forces to form the Vale of Aylesbury. Hardly a pack in the country, except the Duke of Beaufort's and maybe one or two others, was able to carry the number of staff again, so as a result many good men were lost to other professions.

With the major economic problems which have been facing the country for a considerable time now, hunts have been confronting some very difficult decisions about their future. This undoubtedly has had a direct effect on Hunt Staff up and down the land. Couple this with the ban in 2005 and then one could be forgiven for thinking we were on the downward spiral for good. But are we? I don't think so. We do however have to accept, that with constantly changing financial situations, adapting to these is going to be absolutely crucial. Losing experienced and valuable hunt staff who are intent on keeping standards high should not be an option. There is absolutely no room however, in this day and age, for those who believe in keeping a pack of lowland hounds looking like lean mean running machines. It is neither clever to do so, nor acceptable and is a sure sign that the Mastership or the Committee is at fault for allowing it. In some countries the flesh round has ceased to exist, but there is still an adequate amount of other food about to keep hounds looking fit and well, and that must be the priority that is put before anything else.

The resilience of those in Hunt Service is to be admired and respected. In the thirties one would have had to contend with long hacks to and from meets, leaving the kennels at some ungodly hour of the morning. Nowadays with motorised transportation there may not be quite so much time spent in the saddle but kennel duties can go on for longer with reduced manpower to do them. Jobs such as collection of and dealing with fallen stock, and the numerous other tasks that need attending to on a non hunting day, keep hunt staff busy very often until late on in the evening. Keeping the kennels spic and span may well not be their only responsibility. More often than not nowadays, maintenance of the country, which in days gone by would have been the job of either a full time or part time Fencer, is handed over to them. From 2005 having to cope with the iniquitous legislation that was introduced has also added greatly to the pressure on everybody in the profession today.

So, are there really young people out there who are keen to make hunting their life? The answer to that question is yes and it is up to us to encourage them into an occupation that still has a huge amount to offer those who have a natural affiliation with animals. There have always been some wishing to go into the world of hunting and we are now extremely fortunate to have a Bursary scheme, which is run from the Hunting Office, to help them.

This scheme was set up to find, educate and encourage the Huntsmen of the future. In partnership with Haddon Training, an approved training provider specialising in the animal care industry, the Hunting Office has developed a work based learning programme. Much of the course covers the 'Code of Practice for the welfare of hounds in Hunt Kennels' and mirrors what happens in kennels throughout the hunting year. Formalising the training provided in kennels was never going to be easy but it is a good start and it is important to set the bar high as Tim Easby, the Director of the Hunting Office, says when it comes to standards in hunt kennels: "Nothing less than excellent is acceptable". This scheme is open to young people over sixteen who want to be involved with hounds and hunting and not just to those who have spent their early years following hounds. Some of the best candidates are those who until they joined the Bursary had never been near a Hunt Kennels.

To conclude, we have to recognise that we are in an era nowadays of ever changing Masterships and it is vitally important that our Hunt Staff are very much kept in the loop about what is going on. The mutual respect

750 years of Professional Hunt Service at Belvoir

between the two is the key to a hunt's success. Without it one is doomed to failure and internal strife, something with which we certainly do not want to have to contend. Hunt Staff are the glue that keeps the job going on every hunting day and beyond. They are the ones that make the difference between success and failure. Their good manners would put many in this day and age to shame. They turn out our hounds looking fit and well for each hunting day and spend many long hours ensuring that high standards are kept up.

All this is taking place in a world that is constantly watching, observing and waiting to catch us on the wrong foot. So to Hunt Staff up and down the country a deep sense of gratitude is owed to you. Despite everything that has been thrown at us over the years, it is thanks to your guts and determination that we are still able to go out and enjoy our hunting in whatever form it takes.

An Ode to Charlie

Look out young Charlie
Eat food whilst you can,
James Barclay's about,
That dreaded young man.

He's got horses and hounds
And Whipper In too,
You'll know when you see him,
He's not dressed in blue.

Red coat and black hat
And shirt hanging out,
He jumps hedges and ditches
If he knows you're about.

Watch out young Charlie
Eat food while you can,
Read carefully the book
*'See How They Ran!'**

When you hear hounds a coming,
Just sit down and think
How you can dispose
Of that left behind stink!

For if you don't
He'll have your tail,
Hanging up on the wall
By a rusty old nail!

Alfred Jennings
1984

*See How They Ran was written by the late Mary Paul and Juliet Allerton (wife of David Allerton, with whom she was Joint Hon Secretary), about the history of the Essex and Suffolk.

ACKNOWLEDGEMENTS

It was back in 2007 that the idea first came to me about writing a book. At first I did little but jot down bits and pieces about my early life and something of the memorable characters that I had been fortunate enough to meet over the years. As time passed the idea began to grow and then one day I decided to stop dilly dallying about and just get on with it. So that was that, on with it I got and this is the result.

May be taking nearly eight years to write a book is on the slow side but I needed to find a way of writing that would engage you the reader, so that the book would not only be enjoyable but equally interesting. Most importantly if I was going to write a book I was determined to commit to largely illustrating it myself. With the hunting season looming up, I therefore had to look sharp, find a suitable camera and then teach myself how to use it.

When anybody embarks on a project such as this many may think that it is a rather dotty task to undertake, but the ones that stick by you are the ones that really drive you forward. I am forever grateful therefore to my four extremely good friends John Lockwood, John Gardiner, William Craven and Terry Pinner, who have always been a wonderful source of good advice and encouragement. Without their unstinting support I doubt we would have got very far.

Tony Wright, Huntsman of the Exmoor most kindly provided us, from his perspective, details of the strange happenings that took place on the day the Exmoor celebrated the life of Captain Wallace, exactly a year after his death. Tony's knowledge of the country he was hunting and most importantly of the hounds, make the whole piece a fascinating read. Colin Stephenson has been a tower of strength and support to hunting overall but particularly to the Pytchley and before that the Cottesmore. I am so grateful to Colin for writing about what happened after the tragic death of Herbert Norman and the unusual occurrence that took place during a hunt from Langham when the hounds ran back to the very place where poor Herbert had ended his life, before proceeding at a great pace back to his grave.

I would like to record my thanks to John Bycroft for taking the photograph on the front of the dust jacket and for his permission to use it. My deep gratitude also goes to Anne Chown for her trmendous support in helping me write about the remarkable Frank Dallyn.

There are many others who have contributed in different ways to help me create this book. In particular I would like to thank Judith Leman for her wonderful sketches and to Jim Meads for allowing us to use some of his first rate photographs. I must also mention Anona Willows for chauffeuring me about and helping to get me to the right place at the right time enabling me to concentrate on taking the best photos I could. It would be remiss of me to not thank Ian Farquhar and Stephen Lambert for their kind words. Please do forgive me if you think your name should be here and isn't, my sincere gratitude is there all the same.

As you will read both my mother and father had a most profound influence on me, demonstrating the highest standards that need to be set to make our hunting work as it should. My two sons also have great enthusiasm for the "Chase" and this is something that gives my wife and me the greatest of pleasure. Although neither Ben nor Rowley have wished to run after a pack of school beagles or hunt hounds themselves, their knowledge of how it should be done is there and growing all the time. There may well yet come a time when the letters MFH appear after their name as they have with the four generations before them and would I be the one to discourage that? Certainly not! Your support boys, is greatly appreciated.

After three serious accidents my wife Lucy has been determined to live as near normal a life as possible. So to take the time away from her horses to scrutinise this book in her most thorough and diligent way is something for which I will always be indebted to her. Husbands and wives working together on a project such as this is not necessarily designed to create a harmonious atmosphere, however we got through it and here it is.

Thank you Lucy I could not have done it without you.

James Barclay